uCertify Guide for

Microsoft Exam 70-452

MCITP: SQL Server 2008

Pass your MCITP: SQL Server 2008

Certification in first attempt

uCertify Team

www.ucertify.com

Copyright

uCertify Guide for Microsoft Exam 70-452

Foreword

IT certification exams require a lot of study and practice. Many of our customers spend weeks, if not months preparing for the exam. While most classroom training and certification preparation software do a good job of covering exam material and providing practice questions, summarization of the highlights and key study points is often missing.

This book is intended to bridge the gap between preparation and the final exam. It is designed to be an easy reference that will walk you through all the exam objectives with easy to remember key points required to successfully pass the certification exam. It reinforces the key points, while helping you focus on the exam requirements. The benefits are multifold and can help you save hours of exam review, while keeping key concepts fresh in your mind before the exam. This critical review will help you with the final exam preparation touches and give you the confidence needed for the big day.

Benefits of this exam countdown and quick review guide:

1. Focused approach to reviewing exam material – review what you must know

2. All key exam concepts highlighted and reinforced

3. Time saving – must know facts at your finger tips in one condensed version

4. Detailed explanations of all possible answers to practice questions to ensure your grasp of the topic

5. A full length simulation exam to determine your exam readiness.

Table of Contents

How this book will help you

uCertify's guide for Microsoft Exam 70-452 is an invaluable supplement to those in the final stages of their preparation for the Microsoft Exam 70-452 Microsoft SQL Server 2008, Managing Projects.

This book is organized into three sections.

Section A

Section A contains general information about the book and Exam 70-452. It describes the exam objectives, pre-requisites, exam format, test taking tips and strategies and more.

Section B

Section B contains four chapters. Each chapter contains a Quick Review of the material you need to know for a given objective. It reinforces concepts reviewed via Pop Quiz and practice questions.

- **Pop Quiz:** Short, to-the-point questions with definitive answers.

- **Practice Questions:** At the end of each chapter, a series of questions test your understanding of the topics covered in the chapter. These questions are patterned after actual exam questions and difficulty levels. Detailed explanations are provided for each question, explaining not just the correct answer, but the incorrect answers as well, to ensure a real grasp of the question.

Section C

Section C contains fifty-five full-length questions. These questions will test your preparation for the exam within a stipulated period. The Answer Sheet for the exam contains a complete analysis of the question.

Finally, the Appendices includes Acronyms and Glossary followed by References and Index. This is very handy for last minute reviews.

We wish you all the best on your exam!

Principal contributors:
Anurag Dubey
uCertify Team

Section A

Introduction

About uCertify

uCertify is a leading provider of IT certification exam preparation software. For over a decade, we have been preparing top quality preparation guides for over 200 IT certification exams. Our software Preparation Kits (Prepkits, as we call them), contain exhaustive study material, tips, study notes and hundreds of practice questions that culminate in a full length simulated preparation exam. Choose exams from vendors such as Microsoft, Oracle, CompTIA, SUN, CIW, EC-Council, ADOBE, CISCO, ITIL, IBM, LPI, and ISC-2. Authored by highly experienced and certified professionals, uCertify PrepKits not only guarantee your success at getting certified, but also equip you to truly understand the subject.

As they say, "Successful people don't do different things, they do things differently." uCertify's preparation methodology is that difference. We will give you a competitive edge over others who may be paper certified but not qualified to use the skills on the job. A customer pass rate of over 99%, is testimony to the success of our methodology. We guarantee it! Our industry best 100% money back guarantee is second to none! Check it out at:

http://www.ucertify.com/about/guarantee.html

Learn more about us at www.ucertify.com and www.prepengine.com , our smarter learning platform, which powers each of our Prepkits.

About this Book

What this book is and what it's not

This book is invaluable as a final review guide for Microsoft Exam 70-452. It is a supplement to your exam preparation, be it classroom training, practical experience, or even test preparation software. The book is designed to help you save time while ensuring you are ready, by providing you a Quick Review of all exam objectives, without having to review all exam material. In addition, the book helps reinforce key concepts and terminology, both of which are important to review just before your exam. A big bonus is the full length exam simulation practice test that will be a good indicator of your exam readiness.

This book is not a substitute for exhaustive test preparation services such as uCertify Prepkits or classroom training. uCertify strongly recommends that you first study the exam material extensively and gain as much practical experience as possible in the areas you are expected to have skills in. Use this book as a final review before your actual exam.

About Exam 70-452: Microsoft SQL Server 2008

This Microsoft 70-452 exam is designed for IT professionals who are helpful for designing and planning business intelligence (BI) solutions by using Microsoft SQL Server 2008 BI tools. After passing this **70-452 exam**, you earn credit toward the following certification: Microsoft Certified IT Professional (MCITP): Business Intelligence Developer 2008.

Benefits of Certification

IT certification is an industry wide, internationally standardized, highly recognized method that demonstrates your technical problem skills and expertise in a given area. By passing a certification exam, an individual shows to his current or potential employer that she/he recognizes the value of staying current with the latest technology. The certification process helps you gain market relevant skills culminating in an industry respected certificate in one or more areas offered for certification. While not all employers require certification, getting certified is tangible proof of your motivation and skills as an IT professional. Surveys consistently show certified professionals to earn more than their counterparts who do not have a formal certification. Most certified professional have found that their financial investment in training and certification is paid off by gains in salary, job opportunities, or expanded roles, typically over a short period of time.

Exam Registration

Microsoft exams can be registered and taken at Prometric testing centers across the globe. Be sure to give yourself plenty of time to prepare for the exam before you schedule your exam day.

Name	Phone (US and Canada)	Phone Other Countries
Prometric: http://www.prometric.com	1-800-775-3926	1-410-843-8000

Exam Objectives & Skills Expected

Microsoft's 70-452 test validates that an individual has the comprehensive set of skills necessary to perform a particular job role, such as database administrator or enterprise messaging administrator. MCITP certifications are built on the technical proficiency measured in the Microsoft Certified Technology Specialist (MCTS) certifications. Therefore, one can earn one or more MCTS certifications on the way for earning an MCITP credential. Candidates for this exam are IT professionals who design and plan business intelligence (BI) solutions by using Microsoft SQL Server 2008 BI tools.

Microsoft has specified more than thirty objectives for the 70-452 test, which are grouped under six topics. Following are the important areas in which an individual should possess good knowledge before taking the 70-452 test:

- Designing and Managing Reports.

- Accessing report services API.

- Designing a data acquisition strategy.

- Defining a report parameter strategy.

- Designing Data Mining Models.

- Administering a BI Solution.

- Selecting a subscription strategy.

- Making a decision tree.

- Managing data-driven rights.

- Scheduling SSIS packages to run.

- Designing the BI Architecture.

- Selecting BI entry points.

- Designing and Deploying SSIS Packages.

- Designing perspectives.

- Designing an Analysis Services Database.

Who should take this exam?

The test is appropriate for those work or want to work in a typically complex computing environment of medium-to-large organizations. There are no specific prerequisites for this test, although it is recommended that one should have experience in scheduling, estimating, coordinating, controlling, budgeting, and staffing projects and supporting other users of Office Project.

FAQ for Microsoft Exam 70-452

Q. What are the pre-requisites to take the 70-452 exam?

A. There are no specific prerequisites for this test, although it is recommended that one should have experience in scheduling, estimating, coordinating, controlling, budgeting, and staffing projects and supporting other users of Office Project.

Q. What is the 70-452 exam?

A. Microsoft's 70-452 exam (PRO: Designing a Business Intelligence Infrastructure Using Microsoft SQL Server 2008) validates that an individual has the comprehensive set of skills necessary to perform a particular job role, such as database administrator or enterprise messaging administrator.

Q. What are the prerequisites for the 70-452 exam?

A. The prerequisites of this exam are that candidates should have the MCTS certification, about two or three years of experience in managing SQL Server 2008, Business Intelligence Development and Maintenance.

Q. What are the benefits of having an MCITP certification?

A. The benefits of having an MCITP certification are that the MCITP certifications are built on the technical proficiency measured in the Microsoft Certified Technology Specialist (MCTS) certifications. Therefore, one can earn one or more MCTS certifications on the way for earning an MCITP credential. Candidates for this exam are IT professionals who design and plan business intelligence (BI) solutions by using Microsoft SQL Server 2008 BI tools. This test prepares you for various job roles, which include: Business Intelligence Developer 2008, Database Designer, Database Developer, Database Administrator, etc.

Passing Exam 70-452: PRO: Designing a Business Intelligence Infrastructure Using Microsoft SQL Server 2008: counts as credit towards the following certification(s): Microsoft Certified IT Professional (MCITP): Business Intelligence Developer 2008.

Q. What credit does the 70-452 exam provide?

A. Passing the Exam 70-452 : PRO: Designing a Business Intelligence Infrastructure Using Microsoft SQL Server 2008: counts as credit towards the following certification(s): Microsoft Certified IT Professional (MCITP): Business Intelligence Developer 2008.

Q. What certificate does it provide?

A. This exam provides the following certification(s): Microsoft Certified IT Professional (MCITP): Business Intelligence Developer 2008.

Q. How many questions are asked in the test?

A. You will be required to attempt approximately 55 questions.

Q. What is the duration of the test?

A. The duration of the test is 120 minutes.

Q. Which type of test is it? (Adaptive/Linear)

A. It is a Linear test.

Q. What is the passing score?

A. The passing score of the test is 700 out of 1000.

Q. What is the test retake policy?

A. If you do not pass the 70-452 exam in the first attempt, you may take the second shot of the same exam one time without restriction. Second Shot provides a free retake if you do not pass an IT professional or developer Microsoft Certification exam the first time. You must take both the first and (if necessary) the retake exam before June 30, 2010. If you do not achieve a passing score the second time, you must wait at least seven days to retake the test a third time. A 14-day waiting period will be imposed for all subsequent exam retakes. If you have passed an exam, you cannot take it again.

Q. What skills are measured in the 70-452 exam?

A. The following skills are measured in the 70-452 exam:

- Designing and Managing Reports

- Designing Data Mining Models

- Administering a BI Solution

- Designing the BI Architecture

- Designing an Analysis Services Database

Q. Where can I take the test?

A. You can take the exam at the Prometric center.

Test Taking Tips

- Stay calm and be relaxed.

- When you start the test, read the question and ALL its options carefully, even if you think you know the correct answer. Be prepared for the tricky questions!

- If you are taking an adaptive test, remember that you will not get a chance to change your answer once you move on, so be sure before you mark the answer. In a linear test, you will have a chance to change the answer before you hand in the exam.

- If you know the correct answer, attempt the question and move on; if you are not sure, mark your best guess and move on. If it is a linear test, you should also bookmark the question so that you can return to it later.

- Sometimes related questions help you get the right answers for the questions you were unsure of; so, it is always a good idea to bookmark the question.

- If you are unsure of the correct answer, read all the options and eliminate the options that are obviously wrong; then, choose from the options that are left.

- Once you have finished answering all the questions, check the time left. If you have time, review the book-marked questions.

- Never leave a question unanswered. All certification tests that we know are timed and count unanswered questions as wrong. If you don't have time, take a blind guess.

Before the test

- Be confident and relaxed.

- Sleep well the night before the exam.

The Big Day

It is strongly recommended that you arrive at the testing center at least 15 minutes before the exam is scheduled. Don't forget to bring two pieces of identification with you, one of which must be a photo I.D., such as a valid driver's license. You will be required to show the identification when you sign in at the testing center. The center-in-charge will explain the examination rules, after which you will be asked to sign a document that states that you fully understand and abide by the rules of the exam.

Once you are signed in, you will be directed to the exam room. Carrying anything into the room is strictly prohibited. You will be given a few blank pieces of paper and a pen on entering the room. Once you complete the exam, your score will be tabulated and you will know immediately whether you have passed or failed the exam. If you fail, you can retake it as soon as you are ready, even the same day. It is a good idea to note down all the difficult topics you faced during the exam and revise this review guide or other training material before retaking the exam. If you fail the same exam a second time, you must wait at least 14 days before you will be allowed to reschedule.

The testing center-in-charge is typically available to assist with administrative aspects of the testing.

Section B

Core Contents

Chapter 1 - Designing and Managing Reports

Overview

This chapter describes about the section of how to design report architecture, design a data acquisition strategy, design a report layout, and Design reports by using Report Builder.

Design report architecture

- The Schedule tab is used to specify the unit of time (minutes, hours, days, weeks, or months) used by default in the Duration field and the Work field.

- A parameterized report makes use of input values for data processing. Parameterized reports are commonly used for connecting and filtering reports with related data.

- Parameters are used in queries of the dataset to select data of the report, in order to filter the result set that the query returns, or to set layout properties that are used to display or hide parts of a report. For example, a drop-down list of Region parameter values can be used to populate a drop-down list of City parameter values. Reporting Services supports two kinds of parameters: query parameters and report parameters.

- Query parameters are used for selecting or filtering data at the time of processing of data. These are specified in the syntax of a data processing extension. If a query parameter is specified, a value must be provided either by the user or by default properties to complete the SELECT statement or stored procedure that retrieves data for a report.

- Report parameters are used in order to view different aspects of the report data at the time of processing of report. It is generally used to filter a large set of records, but it can also have other uses depending on the queries and expressions used in the report.

- A linked report is an item of the Report Server that supplies an access point to an existing report. Typically, it is analogous to a shortcut that can be used to open a file. A linked report is the derivative of an existing report. It always inherits layout and data source properties from the original report. All other properties may not be the same as that original report including security, parameters, subscriptions, and schedules.

- A snapshot contains information related to layout and query results that were retrieved at a certain time. On-demand reports get up-to-date query results, whereas report snapshots are processed and then saved to a report server on the basis of a schedule. When a snapshot report is selected for viewing, the report server retrieves the stored report from the database and shows the data and layout that were current for the report at the time the snapshot was created.

- An ad hoc report is a report that can be created using an existing report model with the help of Report Builder. These reports refer chiefly to reports of Report Builder and not to reports that can be created with the use of the Report Wizard. Ad hoc reports control report models and pre-defined templates to enable information workers to quickly and easily explore business data using familiar terminology and data structures implemented in the report model. These reports can be saved and run locally or published to a report server, just like other reports in the Reporting Services.

- A clickthrough report is a report that provides detailed information about the contents of the main report. A clickthrough report displays data that is related to a report model. It is displayed when the user clicks the interactive data appearing in the main report. The report server generates these reports automatically based on the information contained in the report model.

- Drillthrough reports are standard reports that are accessed through hyperlinks on a text box in the original report. These reports work with a main report and are the target of a drillthrough action for a report item such as placeholder text or a chart. The main report displays summary information, for example, in a chart. Actions defined in the chart provide drillthrough links to reports that display greater details based on the aggregate in the main report. Drillthrough reports are not displayed within the original report.

- A subreport is similar to a frame in a Web page. A subreport is a report that displays another report inside the body of a main report. In other words, it is used to embed another report within a report. Any report can be used as a subreport. The subreport can use different data sources than the main report. Subreports are typically used within a main report as a briefing book or as a container for a collection of related reports.

- A cube partition allows a user to specify the criteria that are used to split a fact table into multiple pieces for processing. It is defined in order to restructure the processing as well as to improve the processing performance of a cube.

However, a cube partition does not affect the principal storage features of the fact table; instead, it defines the equivalent of a WHERE clause to be used by SQL Server Analysis Services (SSAS) during a processing run.

Once defined, SSAS can process each partition in parallel and then combine the results together.

- The OPENROWSET function in Transact-SQL can be used to pass a connection string and query to a data source to retrieve the required data. If this function is used to retrieve the data from a SQL Server instance, then that instance must be configured to permit ad hoc distributed queries.

The OPENROWSET function can be referenced in the FROM clause of a query as if it were a table name. This function can also be referenced as the target table of an INSERT, UPDATE, or DELETE statement, subject to the capabilities of the OLE DB provider. Although the query might return multiple result sets, OPENROWSET returns only the first one.

Pop Quiz

Q1: In which SQL Server feature is the My Reports role available?

Ans: Report Manager

Q2: Which report is processed on a schedule and then saved to a report server?

Ans: Snapshot reports

Design a data acquisition strategy

- The (All) member is the calculated value of all members in an attribute hierarchy or a user-defined hierarchy. In an MDX query, the (All) member is returned if there is no relationship among the parameters.

- The OPENROWSET function in Transact-SQL can be used to pass a connection string and query to a data source to retrieve the required data. If this function is used to retrieve the data from a SQL Server instance, then that instance must be configured to permit ad hoc distributed queries.

- The OPENROWSET function can be referenced in the FROM clause of a query as if it were a table name. This function can also be referenced as the target table of an INSERT, UPDATE, or DELETE statement, subject to the capabilities of the OLE DB provider. Although the query might return multiple result sets, OPENROWSET returns only the first one.

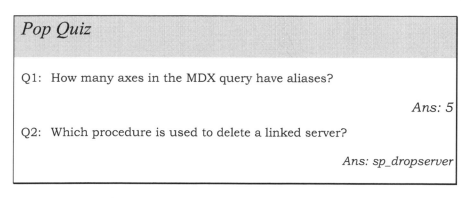

Pop Quiz

Q1: How many axes in the MDX query have aliases?

Ans: 5

Q2: Which procedure is used to delete a linked server?

Ans: sp_dropserver

Define a report parameter strategy

- Report parameters are used to show a different aspect of the data during report processing. A report parameter is normally used to filter a large set of records, but it can have other uses depending on the expressions and queries used in the report. Report parameters in contrast to query parameters are defined in a report and processed by the report server, whereas query parameters are defined as a part of the dataset query and are processed on the database server.

- Cascading parameters are used to manage large amounts of report data. It is possible to define a set of related parameters so that the list of values for one parameter depends on the value chosen in another parameter. As an example, the first parameter is independent and may present a list of product categories. When a category is selected by a user, the second parameter is dependent on the first parameter's value. Its values are updated with the list of subcategories within the chosen category. When the report is viewed by the user, the values for both the category and subcategory parameters are used to filter the report data.

Pop Quiz

Q1: Which language is used to write expressions in Reporting Services?
Ans: Microsoft Visual Basic

Q2: Which expression is used to define a Group by parameter based on user selection?

Ans: =Fields(Parameters!GroupBy.Value).Value

Design a report layout

- The Tablix data region is a universal layout report item that displays report data in cells which are ordered in the form of rows and columns. Report data can be detail data, as it is taken from the data source, or aggregated detail data arranged into groups which are specified by the user. Each Tablix cell can include any report item, such as a text box, or an image.

- The table, matrix, and list data regions are represented in the toolbox by templates for the fundamental Tablix data region. When the user adds one of these templates to a report, he is essentially adding a Tablix data region that is optimized for a particular data layout. As groups for a table, matrix, or list are defined by the user, the Report Designer adds rows and columns to the Tablix data region.

- Data regions are report items that display data rows from the datasets of reports. Data from these datasets can be displayed in the form of a table, matrix, list, chart, or gauge data region. These data regions can be enlarged as needed in order to display the data from the report dataset.

- A user can use a data region to group, sort, filter, and aggregate data from a particular dataset. SQL Server Reporting Services (SSRS) service provides several types of data regions: table, matrix, list, chart, and gauge. The table, matrix, and list data regions templates are based on the Tablix data region. They can be combined in distinctive ways to modify data presentation. Charts present a graphical view of data and aggregates. Gauges present a comparative indicator in a range, such as, for Key Performance Indicators (KPIs).

- The type of data region the user prefers depends on the amount of data, the data value ranges, and what the user wants to express in the report. In order to make the best choice of a data region to display report data, a user should understand the characteristics of your data and the purpose of the report. The following list describes the features of each data region:

  - Table: A table template contains rows and columns. It is used to display detail data, arrange the data in rows, groups, or both. The user can create nested groups or independent, adjacent groups. It produces a predefined set of columns and an unknown number of rows, the number of rows depends upon the content of the dataset. It has three columns with a table header row and a details row. The following figure shows the initial table template, selected on the design surface:

- The table expands down the page as required by the user. He can display all the detail data, row by row, or group the data by forming groups of rows. A row group displays a dynamic row down the page for each value in the group, which is calculated at run-time. These groups can be nested or adjacent. The user can also add static rows for labels or totals. He can add totals to the table or to a specific row group.

- Matrix: The matrix template is used to display aggregated data summaries which are grouped in rows and columns, analogous to a PivotTable or a crosstab. The number of rows and columns for groups can be calculated by the number of unique values for each row and column groups. The following figure shows the initial matrix template, selected on the design surface:

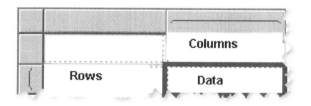

A matrix has at least one row group and one column group. It can expand across the page for column groups and down the page for row groups. The matrix cells display summary and aggregate values which are scoped to the intersections of the row and column groups. The user can generate extra nested groups and adjacent groups. The number of rows and columns in a matrix depend on the values for each group, determined at run-time. The user can also add static rows for labels or totals.

The list template is used to create a free-form layout. For example, a list can be used to design a form or display both a table and a chart. Arrange text boxes anywhere in the list to create your layout. The list row repeats one time for each value in the dataset.

The user is not limited to a grid layout, but can place fields freely inside the list. He can use a list to design a form in order to display many dataset fields or as a container to display multiple data regions side by side for grouped data. For example, the user can define a group for a list; add a table, chart, and image; and display values in table and graphic form for each group value. The list template does not deals with columns and rows. This feature makes it a good choice to make a report that is intended to resemble a form.

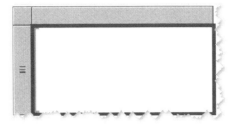

- Chart: A chart is used to display the report data graphically. Charts help the user to visualize summary and aggregate data.

- Gauge: A gauge displays an indicator in the range of data values. These can be used in a table or matrix in order to show the relative value of a field in a range of values in the data region, for example, as a KPI. The user can also add a gauge for designing a surface showing a single relative value.

Pop Quiz

Q1: What is the default name of the console application's code file in an RDL Visual Studio project?

Ans: Program.cs

Q2: Which class is used to write Report Definition Language to a report definition file using the .NET Framework?

Ans: System.Xml.XmlTextWriter class

Design reports by using Report Builder

- The Report designer is a set of graphical tools and windows that run within Visual Studio 2005. The Report Designer can be launched from BIDS or from Visual Studio 2005 if it is already installed. Report designer is used to create reports, which can be connected to a data source. Data is retrieved on the basis of queries. Reports can also be created through the Report Wizard and modified in the design view. When a Report project or Report Wizard project template is selected, the Report Designer data and design surface appears. A query designer and an expression editor are included in the Report Designer.

- A report project acts as a container for report resources and definitions. When the project is deployed, every file in the report project is published to the report server. When the project is created for the first time, a solution is also created as a container for the project. Multiple projects can be added to a single solution. A connection is then defined to the data source that users want to use for their report and define the dataset for the report. After defining the data for the report, layout and interactive features can be designed.

- Report Manager is a Web-based report access and management tool that can be used to administer a single report server instance from a remote location over an HTTP connection. Report Manager can also be used for its report viewer and navigation features.

- Business Intelligence Development Studio (BIDS) is Microsoft Visual Studio 2008 with additional project types that are specific to SQL Server business intelligence. BIDS is the main environment that a user will use to develop business solutions that include Integration Services, Analysis Services, and Reporting Services projects. Business Intelligence Development Studio is basically a development tool that is used to create reports, packages, and analysis projects. This tool contains projects and wizards to create the reports, packages and analysis projects either automatically or manually.

Pop Quiz

Q1: What task of the Report Builder role definition is used to read report definitions?

Ans: Consume reports

Q2: Which data region is used by the SQL Server Reporting Services to define a report format that supports row and column groups?

Ans: Matrix

Manage a report environment

- The Report Manager is a Web-based tool that can be used in Native Mode to access and administer the Reporting Services over the Web. With

Report Manager, administrators can carry out a wide range of tasks including viewing and managing reports and subscriptions, configuring report processing options, configuring security from any computer with a browser, etc.

- Activity Monitor is a tool in SQL Server Management Studio (SSMS). It is used to get information about user connections to the database engine. It is also used to troubleshoot database locking issues and to terminate deadlocked or unresponsive processes.

Pop Quiz

Q1: Which installation option instructs Setup to use default values when installing a report server?

Ans: Install the default configuration

Q2: Which mode is used by the Report Manager?

Ans: Native mode

Test Your Knowledge

Q1.   Which of the following parameters of the report server are defined as part of the dataset query and processed on the database server?

   A. Report parameter

   B. Query parameter

   C. Cascading parameter

   D. Default parameter

Q2.   You work as an Administrator for TechMart Inc. The company has a SQL Server 2008 computer. You manage a SQL Server 2008 Reporting Services (SSRS) solution. The report server in SSRS is running in native mode. You have created the report project and want to publish some items in a project with the help of the Report Designer. Data source is present on the server and you want to overwrite the data source on the server each time the reports are published. Which of the following are necessary to set the deployment properties?

   Each correct answer represents a part of the solution. Choose all that apply.

   A.   You should select True in the OverwriteDataSources.

   B.   You must have Publish permissions on the target folder to publish reports to that folder.

   C.   You should use the URL of the virtual directory of the report server.

   D.   You must have Member or Owner permission on the SharePoint site.

   E.   You should select False in the OverwriteDataSources.

Q3.   You work as a Developer for Bluewell Inc. The company has a SQL Server 2008 computer. You are designing a Microsoft SQL Server 2008 Reporting Services (SSRS) accounting report. You want every alternate row of the output in the report table to have a green background. You need to use the appropriate expression for the BackgroundColor property of the table. Which of the following expressions should you choose to accomplish the task?

   A.   =Iif((RowNumber(Nothing)),"Green","Orange")

B.   =Iif((RowNumber(Nothing)),"Green","White")

C.   =Iif((RowNumber(Nothing) MOD 2),"Green","White")

D.   =Iif((RowNumber),"Green","Orange")

Q4. You work as a Developer for Softech Inc. The company has a SQL Server 2008 computer. You are designing a Microsoft SQL Server 2008 Reporting Services (SSRS) sales report. You want to design the report in a flexible manner, i.e., if the number of items increases and there is a need to grow the report, you are able to make the report flexible. How will peer items be shifted when any item such as a table is added to the report?

Each correct answer represents a complete solution. Choose all that apply.

A.   Each item will move down to maintain minimum spacing between itself and all the items ending above it.

B.   Each item will move to the right to maintain minimum spacing between itself and the items ending to the left of it.

C.   Each item will move up to maintain minimum spacing between itself and all the items ending below it.

D.   Each item will move to the left to maintain minimum spacing between itself and the items ending to the right of it.

Q5. Which of the following properties of the ProjectName property page dialog box allows users to configure the report that will be automatically displayed when running the project for debugging purposes?

A.   StartItem

B.   OverWriteDataSources

C.   TargetDataSourceFolder

D.   TargetReportFolder

E.   TargetServerURL

Answer Explanation

A1.   Answer option B is correct.

Query parameters are used during data processing to filter or select data. These parameters are specified in the syntax of a data processing extension. If a query parameter is specified, either a user or the default properties should provide a value to complete the SELECT statement or stored procedure that retrieves data for a report.

Answer option A is incorrect. Report parameters are used to show a different aspect of the data during report processing. A report parameter is normally used to filter a large set of records, but it can have other uses depending on the expressions and queries used in the report. Report parameters in contrast to query parameters are defined in a report and processed by the report server, whereas query parameters are defined as a part of the dataset query and are processed on the database server.

Answer option C is incorrect. Cascading parameters are used to manage large amounts of report data. It is possible to define a set of related parameters so that the list of values for one parameter depends on the value chosen in another parameter. As an example, the first parameter is independent and may present a list of product categories. When a category is selected by a user, the second parameter is dependent on the first parameter's value. Its values are updated with the list of subcategories within the chosen category. When the report is viewed by the user, the values for both the category and subcategory parameters are used to filter the report data.

Answer option D is incorrect. There is no such parameter as default parameter.

A2.   Answer options A, B, and C are correct.

Following are the steps to set the deployment properties in the report project:

Right-click the report project, and then click Properties.

Select a configuration to edit from the configuration list in the Property Pages dialog box for the project.

In StartItem, select a report to display in the preview window or in a browser window when the report project is run.

In OverwriteDataSources, select False to keep the data source on the server and True to overwrite the data source on the server each time reports are published.

In the TargetDataSourceFolder text box, type the folder on the report server in which to place the published shared data sources.

In the TargetReportFolder text box, type the folder on the report server in which to place the published reports.

In the TargetServerURL text box, the URL of the target report server should be typed. The URL of the virtual directory of the report server should be used when publishing to a report server running in the native mode.

Note: This is the virtual directory of the report server, not Report Manager. When publishing to a report server running in the SharePoint integrated mode, a URL to a SharePoint top-level site or subsite should be used .

A3.   Answer option C is correct.

You should choose the =Iif((RowNumber(Nothing) MOD 2),"Green","White") expression to accomplish the task.

The Iif function is used to return one of two values depending on whether the expression evaluated is true or not. The following expression uses the Iif function to return a Boolean value of True if the value of LineCount exceeds 50. Otherwise it returns False:

=Iif(Fields!LineCount.Value > 50, True, False)

The RowNumber function is used to number the rows in a table. This function is also useful for more complex tasks, like providing page breaks based on the number of rows. An expression containing the RowNumber function, when used in a text box within a data region displays the row number for every instance of the text box in which the expression appears. The Nothing keyword indicates that the function will begin counting at the first row in the outermost data region.

MOD stands for modulus (%) operator. It is used to find out the remainder after a division has been completed. Since MOD 2 is mentioned in the argument, the line number will get divided by 2, and if the remainder is 0, i.e., the number is completely divided by 2, the output background will be green; otherwise it will remain white.

Answer option B is incorrect. The =Iif((RowNumber(Nothing)),"Green","White") expression will make the background color of every row green, whereas it is stated in the question that every alternate row of the output in the report table should have a green background.

Answer option A is incorrect. The =Iif((RowNumber(Nothing)),"Green","Orange") expression will alternate the background color of each row between green and orange. This is not required according to the question.

Answer option D is incorrect. It is mentioned in the question that the background of every alternate row should be green; therefore, the 'Nothing' function with MOD 2 operator is necessary to accomplish the task. The =Iif((RowNumber),"Green","Orange") expression will not serve the purpose.

A4.   Answer options A and B are correct.

There are three main areas in a report: the page header, page footer, and the body. Freeform placement of the report items in a report is supported by the Reporting Services. When reports are being designed, it is necessary to understand how the items will behave if they grow. Depending on the section repeats and content size, the items in a report may grow either horizontally or vertically.

When an item grows, it pushes peer items out of the way. Items within the same parent container are called peer items. Following are the two ways in which the peer items are shifted:

Each item moves down to maintain minimum spacing between itself and all the items ending above it.

Each item moves to the right to maintain minimum spacing between itself and the items ending to the left of it.

A5.   Answer option A is correct.

The StartItem property of the ProjectName property page dialog box allows users to configure the report that will be automatically displayed when running the project for debugging purposes.

Answer option B is incorrect. The OverWriteDataSources property is used to replace the shared data sources in the deployment server when it is set to Yes.

Answer option C is incorrect. The TargetDataSourceFolder property represents the folder in which a shared data source will be deployed.

Answer option D is incorrect. The TargetReportFolder property represents the folder in which a report will be deployed.

Answer option E is incorrect. The TargetServerURL property represents the URL of the deployment server.

Chapter 2 - Designing Data Mining Models

Overview

This chapter describes about the section of how to design a mining model and structure, design strategies for staging data for mining, select a strategy for visualizing data mining results, select data mining algorithms, refine testing models, and refine testing models.

Design a mining model and structure

- The sp_help_fulltext_system_components stored procedure is used to retrieve information about the registered word-breakers, filters, and protocol handlers.

  Syntax:

  sp_help_fulltext_system_components

  { 'all' | [@component_type =] 'component_typc' }

  , [@param =] 'param'

  Arguments:

  'all': This argument returns the information for all full-text components.

  [@component_type =] component_type: This argument specifies the type of component.

  [@param =] param: Based on component type, this can be one of the following: a locale identifier (LCID), the file extension with "." prefix, the full component name of the protocol handler, or the full path to the component DLL.

  The SP_FULLTEXT_SERVICE procedure is used to rctrieve information related to the properties of the Full-Text Engine and to change the properties for the MS Full-Text Search service.

  Syntax:

  sp_fulltext_service [[@action=] 'action'

  [, [@value=] value]]

  Arguments:

[@action=] 'action': It is the property to be changed or reset.

[@value=] value: It is the value of the specified property.

The SP_HELP_FULLTEXT_TABLES stored procedure returns a list of tables that are registered for full-text indexing.

Syntax:

sp_help_fulltext_tables   [[@fulltext_catalog_name   =   ] 'fulltext_catalog_name']

[, [@table_name =] 'table_name']

Arguments:

[@fulltext_catalog_name =] 'fulltext_catalog_name': It is the full-text catalog name. fulltext_catalog_name is sysname, with a default value NULL.

If fulltext_catalog_name is omitted or is NULL, all full-text indexed tables that are associated with the database are returned. If fulltext_catalog_name is specified, but table_name is omitted or is NULL, the full-text index information is retrieved for every full-text indexed table that is associated with this catalog. If both fulltext_catalog_name and table_name are specified, a row is returned if table_name is associated with fulltext_catalog_name; otherwise, an error is raised.

- [@table_name =] 'table_name': It is the name of the one- or two-part table for which the full-text metadata is requested.

- The mining structure is a data structure that defines the data domain from which mining models are built. Multiple mining models that share the same domain can be present in a single mining structure. Columns are the building blocks of the mining structure. These columns describe the data contained in the data source and contain information such as content type, data type, and how the data is distributed. A mining structure can also contain nested tables, which represent a one-to-many relationship between the entity of a case and its related attributes. The information about how columns are used for a specific mining model, or about the type of algorithm used to build a model, is not present in the mining structure.

> ## *Pop Quiz*
>
> Q1: Which data mining processing option reads and cashes the training data in the structure?
>
> *Ans: . Process Structure*
>
> Q2: What is TRUE about the packages when a data source is no longer a part of the project?
>
> *Ans: The packages continue to be valid*

Design strategies for staging data for mining.

- A staging area is a place to hold temporary tables on a data warehouse server. The staging area is mostly needed to hold the data, and to carry out data cleansing and merging, before loading the data into the warehouse. Having a staging area decouples the extraction processes from operational processes. This serves to reduce the load placed on the source systems by the extraction processes. Moreover, using staging areas allows multiple source systems to increase performance which can act as an integration point prior to the processing of transformations.

- The process of extracting authentic, valid, and actionable information from a larger database is known as data mining. This means data mining derives trends and patterns that exist in data, which can be collected together and defined as a mining model. Some specific business scenarios where mining models can be applied are as follows:

  - Forecasting sales

  - Predicting the products that are likely to be sold together

  - Targeting mailings toward particular customers

  - Finding the sequence in which customers add products to a shopping cart

- A table in a data source view can be replaced with a different table from the same or a different data source by the Data Source View Designer feature of SQL Server 2008. When a table is replaced, all other objects in the SSAS database or project having references to the table continue to reference it because the object ID for the table in the data source view remains the same.

- On the other hand, if the user deletes and then adds a table, all the references and relationships are lost and must be recreated. To replace a table with another table, the user must have an active connection to the source data in the Data Source View Designer in project mode.

- Preparing data is the second step in the data mining process. In this step, data is consolidated and cleaned that was identified in the first (Defining the problem) step of the data mining process. Microsoft SQL Server Integration Services (SSIS) contains all tools that are required to complete this step, including transforms to automate data cleaning and consolidation. Data can be scattered across a company, stored in different formats, or may contain flawed or missing entries. These problems should be fixed before the models are started to be built.

- Exploring data is the third step in the data mining process in which the prepared data is explored. A user must understand the data in order to make appropriate decisions when the models are created. Exploring techniques include calculating mean and standard deviations, calculating the minimum and maximum values, and looking at the distribution of data. After the data is explored, a user can decide whether the dataset contains flawed data, and then a strategy could be devised for fixing the problems.

- Building models is the fourth step in the data mining process. Before building a model, the prepared data must be randomly separated into separate training and testing datasets. The knowledge achieved from the third (Exploring Data) step of the data mining process is used to define and create a mining model. A model typically contains an identifying column, a predictable column, and input columns.

  After the structure of the mining model is defined, it is processed, which populates the empty structure with the patterns that describe the model. This is known as training the model. A data mining structure object, a data mining algorithm, and a data mining model object are used to define a mining model.

- Exploring and Validating Models is the fifth step in the data mining process in which the models that have already been built are explored and their effectiveness is tested. It is not a wise decision to deploy a model in a production environment without even testing its performance. Moreover, as more than one model may have been created, the user will have to decide which model performs the best. If none of the created models perform well, the previous steps of the data mining process are again carried out either by redefining the problem or by reinvestigating the data in the original dataset.

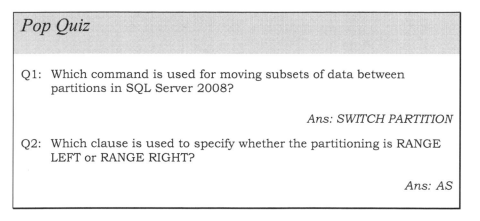

Pop Quiz

Q1: Which command is used for moving subsets of data between partitions in SQL Server 2008?

Ans: SWITCH PARTITION

Q2: Which clause is used to specify whether the partitioning is RANGE LEFT or RANGE RIGHT?

Ans: AS

Select data mining algorithms. Refine testing models.

- The SAMPLE_SIZE parameter of the clustering algorithm specifies the number of cases that is used by the algorithm on each pass if the parameter of the CLUSTERING_METHOD is set to one of the scalable clustering methods. If the SAMPLE_SIZE parameter is set to 0, it will cause the whole dataset to be clustered in a single pass, which may cause memory and performance issue. The default value of the SAMPLE_SIZE is 50000.

- The CLUSTER_COUNT parameter is used to specify the approximate number of clusters that a clustering algorithm should build. The algorithm builds as many clusters as possible if the approximate number of clusters cannot be built from the data. The default value of CLUSTER_COUNT is 10. If the value is set to 0, it causes the algorithm to use heuristic to determine the number of clusters to build.

- The MODELLING_CARDINALITY parameter of the Clustering algorithm is used to specify the number of sample models that are constructed during the clustering process. If the number of candidate models is reduced, it may improve the performance at the risk of missing some good quality models. The default value of this parameter is 10.

- The STOPPING_TOLERANCE parameter of the Clustering algorithm specifies the value that is used to find out when convergence is attained and when the algorithm has finished building the model. When the overall change in cluster probabilities is less than the ratio of the STOPPING_TOLERANCE parameter divided by the size of the model, the convergence is reached. The default value of this parameter is 10.

- The Decision Trees algorithm is the most popular data mining algorithm, which is used to predict discrete and continuous variables. The reason that this algorithm is so popular is that the results generated are very easy to understand by the user. If a user predicts continuous variables, he gets piecewise multiple linear regression formulae with separate formulae in each node of a tree. The discrete input variables are used by the algorithm to split the tree into nodes. A tree that predicts continuous variables is a Regression Tree.

- The Naive Bayes data mining algorithm is used to calculate the probabilities for each possible state of the input attribute, provided that each state of the predictable attribute is given. These probabilities can be used later to predict an outcome of the target attribute that a user is predicting, based on the known input attributes. This algorithm is very simple and is capable of building the models very quickly. Therefore, this algorithm can be used by users as a starting point in their prediction task. The Naive Bayes algorithm does not support continuous attributes.

- The Association Rules data mining algorithm is designed for the market basket analysis. The algorithm defines an itemset as a combination of items in a single transaction. The algorithm scans the dataset and counts the number of times the itemsets appear in the transactions. This algorithm should be used for detecting the cross-selling opportunities.

- The clustering algorithm is a segmentation algorithm provided by SQL Server 2008 Analysis Services (SSAS). This is an iterative algorithm that groups cases in a dataset into clusters with similar characteristics. These groupings are useful for exploring data, identifying anomalies in the data, and creating predictions.

For example, consider a group of people who share similar demographic information and who buy similar products from the Adventure Works company. This group of people represents a cluster of data. Several such clusters may exist in a database. By observing the columns that make up a cluster, one can more clearly see how records in a dataset are related to one another.

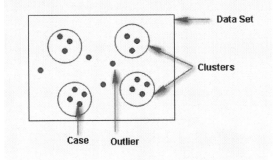

Pop Quiz

Q1: Which is used as a data tracking feature in SQL Server 2008?

Ans: Change Data Capture (CDC)

Q2: Which Data Definition statement is used to add a mining model to an existing mining structure?

Ans: ALTER MINING STRUCTURE

Refine testing models

- The MINIMUM_SUPPORT parameter is used to indicate the minimum size of each node in a decision tree. For example, if this value is set to 15, any split that would produce a child node having less than 15 cases is not accepted. The default value for MINIMUM_SUPPORT in SQL Server 2008 is 10.

- The value of the COMPLEXITY_PENALTY parameter is a floating point number within the range [0,1]. When the value of this parameter is set close to 0, there is a lower penalty for the growth of the decision tree. When its value is set close to 1, the tree growth is penalized heavily, and the resulting trees are relatively small.

- The SPLIT_METHOD parameter is used to specify the shape of a decision tree. This procedure can take the following values:

  SPLIT_METHOD=1 means that the decision tree is split only in a binary way.

  SPLIT_METHOD=2 means that the decision tree is split completely on each attribute (bushy way).

  SPLIT_METHOD=3 means that the decision tree will automatically choose the better of the two above methods to create the split.

  The default value of the SPLIT_METHOD is 3.

Pop Quiz

Q1: Which data mining algorithm is used to predict discrete and continuous variables?

Ans: Decision Trees

Q2: Which data mining algorithm predicts one or more discrete variables, based on the other attributes in the dataset?

Ans: Classification Algorithms

Maintain server health

- Dynamic Management Views (DMVs) are system views that surface the internal counters of the database engine. These views also help the user to present an easily comprehendible dashboard of the database engine performance that can be used to examine the health of a server instance, diagnose problems, etc.

- BIDS (Business Intelligence Development Studio) is a development tool used to create reports, packages, and analysis projects. It is a part of Visual Studio 2005. The tool contains projects and wizards to create the reports, packages and analysis projects either automatically or manually.

- A business intelligence solution is used to present data in a variety of ways, such as dashboards, scorecards, and reports. Data visualization is a key aspect of business intelligence and a proper use of these techniques is the best way to make reports in SQL more useful and effective.

- The Report Server temporary database is used by each report server database to store execution data and session, cached reports, and tables that are generated by the report server. By default, the temporary database is named as reportservertempdb. If the temporary database is missing, it is not recreated by the Reporting Services. Although the temporary database does not contain persisted data, it is recommended that a backup copy of the temporary database be taken. This is done mainly to avoid the recreation of the temporary database as part of a failure recovery operation.

- Microsoft SQL Server 2008 provides a scalable enterprise data integration platform with excellent Extract, Transform, Load (ETL), and integration capabilities. These capabilities facilitate organizations to handle data from a wide range of data sources. This data is converted into an Integration Services data type when it enters a data flow in a package. If data has a data type that is not convertible to an Integration Services data type, an error occurs.

- Numeric data is allocated a numeric data type, string data is allocated a character data type, and dates are allocated a date data type. Other data, such as GUIDs and Binary Large Object Blocks (BLOBs), are also allocated suitable Integration Services data types.

- SSIS (SQL Server Integration Services) is an upgrade of DTS (Data Transformation Services), which is a feature of the previous version of SQL Server. SSIS packages can be created in BIDS (Business Intelligence Development Studio). These can be used to merge data from heterogeneous data sources into SQL Server. They can also be used to populate data warehouses, to clean and standardize data, and to automate administrative tasks.

Pop Quiz

Q1: What is used to present data in a variety of ways, such as dashboards, scorecards, and reports?

Ans: business intelligence solution

Q2: What is an upgrade of DTS (Data Transformation Services), which is a feature of the previous version of SQL Server?

Ans: SSIS

Design a backup strategy.

- The full recovery model makes use of log backups to avoid data loss in the broadest range of failure events. In this case, backing and restoring the log backups is needed. The benefit of using log backups is that the database can be restored to any point of time that is contained within a log backup. Log backups can be used in a sequence to roll a database forward to any point of time that is contained in one of the transaction logs.

- A partial backup is designed to be used under the simple recovery model to improve flexibility for backing up very large databases, which consist of one or more read-only file groups. A partial backup resembles a full database backup. It contains all the data in the primary file group, every read/write file group, and read-only files that are specified optionally. A partial backup is useful whenever read-only file groups are needed to be excluded.

- The Database Engine is the underlined component of a database. It is a collection of information stored on the computer in a systematic way. It is mainly used for storing, securing, and processing data in the database. The Database Engine ensures controlled access and rapid transaction processing to meet the requirements of the most demanding data consuming applications in any organization. SQL Server supports up to fifty instances of the Database Engine on one computer.

Pop Quiz

Q1: What is a collection of information stored on the computer in a systematic way?

Ans: Database Engine

Q2: What is designed to be used under the simple recovery model to improve flexibility for backing up very large databases, which consist of one or more read-only file groups?

Ans: Partial backup

Plan and manage upgrades.

- The Parallel processing setting is used for batch processing. This setting causes Analysis Services to fork off processing tasks to execute in parallel inside a single transaction. If a failure occurs, the result generated is a rollback of all changes. A user can set the maximum number of parallel tasks, or allow the server to decide the optimal distribution. The Parallel processing option is useful for speeding up the processing.

- SQL Server 2008 Upgrade Advisor helps a user to prepare for upgrades to SQL Server 2008. It generates reports after analyzing the previously installed SQL Server 2005, SQL Server 2000, or SQL Server 7.0. On the basis of the report generated, the issues that have to be fixed are identified either before or after the upgrade to SQL Server 2008. The Upgrade Advisor Home page appears when Upgrade Advisor is run. The tools that could be run from the home page are as follows:

  - Upgrade Advisor Analysis Wizard

  - Upgrade Advisor Report Viewer

• Upgrade Advisor Help

Pop Quiz

Q1: What helps a user to prepare for upgrades to SQL Server 2008?

Ans: SQL Server 2008 Upgrade Advisor

Q2: What is used for batch processing?

Ans: Parallel processing setting

Plan and manage reporting services configuration

• The sp_configure stored procedure is used to display or change global configuration settings for the current server. The ALTER DATABASE statement and the SET statement are used to change database-level settings and settings that affect only the current user session, respectively. The syntax of sp_configure is as follows:

sp_configure [[@configname =] 'option_name'

[, [@configvalue =] 'value']]

where,

[@configname =] 'option_name' is the name of a configuration option. option_name is varchar(35), with a default of NULL. The SQL Server Database Engine identifies any unique string that is part of the configuration name. A complete list of options is returned if no string is specified.

[@configvalue =] 'value' is the new configuration setting. value is int, with a default of NULL.

• A Database Mail profile is an ordered collection of related Database Mail accounts. In order to send mail, a user must be a member of the DatabaseMailUserRole in the msdb database, and should have access to at least one Database Mail profile. Profiles permit database administrators to reconfigure stored procedures and database applications that use e-mail without changing the application code. For example, a profile can be configured with one set of e-mail accounts during application development and testing, and then be updated with another set of accounts when the application shifts to production. The application uses the same profile name, but sends e-mail using a different list of e-mail servers.

- The sp_send_dbmail stored procedure is used to send an e-mail message to the specified recipients. The message may include file attachments, a query result set, or both. It returns the mailitem_id of the message when the mail is successfully placed in the Database Mail queue. This stored procedure is in the msdb database. The execute permissions for sp_send_dbmail default to all members of the DatabaseMailUser database role in the msdb database.

- The Reporting Services Configuration tool is used to configure a Reporting Services installation. If a report server is installed by using the files-only installation option, this tool should be used to configure the server before it is used. If the default configuration installation option is used to install a report server, this tool can be used to modify or verify the settings that were specified during the setup. Reporting Services Configuration can be used to configure a remote or local server instance.

- The SQL Server Configuration Manager is a tool used to manage the services associated with SQL Server. It can be used to configure network connections, network protocols, and network libraries. The SQL Server Configuration Manager is a Microsoft Management Console snap-in that is available from the Start menu. It uses Windows Management Instrumentation (WMI) to view and change some server settings.

- A configuration is a set of property-value pairs that are used to define the properties of the package and its containers, tasks, variables, event-handlers, and connections when the package executes. It is possible to update properties without modifying the package by using configurations.

- When the package is executed, the configuration information is loaded as a result of which the values of properties get updated. For example, the connection string of connection can be updated with the help of a configuration. When the package is installed on a different computer, the configuration is saved and then deployed with the package. To support the package in a different environment, the values in the configuration can be updated when the package is installed.

- Database Mail is used for sending e-mail messages from the Microsoft SQL Server 2005 and 2008 Database Engine. It can be used by database applications to send e-mail messages to users. The messages may include results of the query, and can also contain files from any resource on the user's network. Database Mail is designed for reliability, scalability, security, and supportability. It provides a robust, high-performance replacement for the most commonly requested features of SQL Mail. Database Mail is designed to function with SMTP servers.

- SQL Mail provides a way to receive e-mail messages generated by SQL Server. These messages can be triggered to provide the status of a job or a warning caused by an alert. SQL Mail can include a result set in reply to e-mail messages that contain queries. SQL Mail allows SQL Server to send and receive e-mails by establishing a client connection with a mail server. SQL Server uses two services to handle mail, MSSQLServer and SQLAgentMail.

- Database Mail can be enabled using either the sp_configure stored procedure or the Database Mail Configuration Wizard. Additionally, the Database Mail Configuration Wizard can be used to create a Database Mail profile. Once it is enabled and a profile has been created, the sp_send_dbmail stored procedure can be used to send emails.

- Reporting Services Configuration Manager can enable and name the virtual directories for the report server and Report Manager after the installation.

- A configuration is a set of property-value pairs that defines the properties of the package and its tasks, containers, variables, connections, and event handlers when the package runs.

- The Build package verification option is used to specify the sequential Build number associated with the build.

- The Reporting Services Configuration Manager tool can be used to change or create the virtual directories for the report server and Report Manager after installation.

Pop Quiz

Q1: What is used to specify the sequential Build number associated with the build?

Ans: Build package verification option

Q2: Which can be used to change or create the virtual directories for the report server and Report Manager after installation?

Ans: Reporting Services Configuration Manager tool

Test Your Knowledge

Q1. Which of the following features of SQL Server 2008 can be used by a Database Administrator to prevent the usage of the clustering algorithm for data mining?

    A.   SQL Server Analysis Services (SSAS)

    B.   SQL Server Reporting Services (SSRS)

    C.   SQL Server Integration Services (SSIS)

    D.   SQL Server Management Studio (SSMS)

Q2. You work as an Administrator for TechMart Inc. The company has a SQL Server 2008 computer. You are managing SQL Server 2008 Analysis Services (SSAS). You want to create a session mining model. Which of the following properties should you choose to accomplish the task?

    A.   AllowSessionMiningModels

    B   AllowAdHocOpenRowsetQueries

    C   AllowedProvidersInOpenRowset

    D   MaxConcurrentPredictionQueries

Q3. Which of the following parameters are used to limit the depth of a decision tree in data mining?

Each correct answer represents a complete solution. Choose all that apply.

    A.   FORCE_REGRESSOR

    B.   SPLIT_METHOD

    C.   MINIMUM_SUPPORT

    D.   COMPLEXITY_PENALTY

Q4. Which of the following data mining algorithms is appropriate for fraud detection?

    A.   Association rules algorithm

    B.   Clustering algorithm

    C.   Decision Trees algorithm

D.   Naive Bayes algorithm

Q5.   Which of the following data mining algorithms is used to calculate the probabilities for each possible state of the input attribute, provided that each state of the predictable attribute is given?

A.   Naive Bayes

B.   Decision Trees

C.   Association Rules

D.   Clustering

Answer Explanation

A1.   Answer option D is correct.

The clustering algorithm can be disabled by using the Analysis Services Properties dialog box in SQL Server Management Studio. SQL Server Management Studio (SSMS) is a combination of various graphical tools such as Query Analyzer, Enterprise Manager, and Analysis Manager. SSMS is used to access, configure, manage, administer, and develop all the objects and components of SQL Server.

Answer option A is incorrect. SSAS stands for SQL Server Analysis Services. It stores, processes, and secures data. It delivers OLAP (Online Analytical Processing) and data mining functionalities for business intelligence applications. It is used to design, create, and manage multi-dimensional structures that contain data aggregated from other data sources.

Answer option B is incorrect. The SQL Server Reporting Services (SSRS) is a server-based reporting platform that can be used to create and manage tabular, graphical, matrix, and free-form reports that contain data from multidimensional and relational data sources. The report that is created can be viewed and managed over a World Wide Web-based connection.

Answer option C is incorrect. SSIS (SQL Server Integration Services) is an upgrade of DTS (Data Transformation Services), which is a feature of the previous version of SQL Server. SSIS packages can be created in BIDS (Business Intelligence Development Studio). These can be used to merge data from heterogeneous data sources into SQL Server. They can also be used to populate data warehouses, to clean and standardize data, and to automate administrative tasks.

A2.   Answer option A is correct.

AllowSessionMiningModels is a Boolean property that indicates whether session mining models can be created or not. False is the default value for this property, which implies that session mining models cannot be created.

Answer option B is incorrect. AllowAdHocOpenRowsetQueries is a Boolean property that indicates whether adhoc open rowset queries are allowed or not. False is the default value for this property, which implies that open rowset queries are not allowed during a session.

Answer option C is incorrect. AllowedProvidersInOpenRowset is a string property that identifies which providers are allowed in an open rowset. It consists of a semi-colon/comma separated list of provider ProgIDs, or else [All].

Answer option D is incorrect. MaxConcurrentPredictionQueries is a signed 32-bit integer property that is used to define the maximum number of concurrent prediction queries.

A3.   Answer options C and D are correct.

The MINIMUM_SUPPORT parameter is used to indicate the minimum size of each node in a decision tree. For example, if this value is set to 15, any split that would produce a child node having less than 15 cases is not accepted. The default value for MINIMUM_SUPPORT in SQL Server 2008 is 10.

The value of the COMPLEXITY_PENALTY parameter is a floating point number within the range [0,1]. When the value of this parameter is set close to 0, there is a lower penalty for the growth of the decision tree. When its value is set close to 1, the tree growth is penalized heavily, and the resulting trees are relatively small.

Answer option A is incorrect. The FORCE_REGRESSOR parameter is used to override the regressor selection logic in a decision tree algorithm and forces the regressor to use specific attributes. This parameter is generally used in price elasticity models.

Answer option B is incorrect. The SPLIT_METHOD parameter is used to specify the shape of a decision tree. This procedure can take the following values:

SPLIT_METHOD=1 means that the decision tree is split only in a binary way.

SPLIT_METHOD=2 means that the decision tree is split completely on each attribute (bushy way).

SPLIT_METHOD=3 means that the decision tree will automatically choose the better of the two above methods to create the split.

The default value of the SPLIT_METHOD is 3.

A4.   Answer option B is correct.

The clustering algorithm is used for fraud detection.

The clustering algorithm is a segmentation algorithm provided by SQL Server 2008 Analysis Services (SSAS). This is an iterative algorithm that groups cases in a dataset into clusters with similar characteristics. These groupings are useful for exploring data, identifying anomalies in the data, and creating predictions.

For example, consider a group of people who share similar demographic information and who buy similar products from the Adventure Works company. This group of people represents a cluster of data. Several such clusters may exist in a database. By observing the columns that make up a cluster, one can more clearly see how records in a dataset are related to one another.

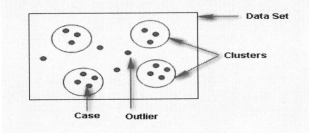

Answer option A is incorrect. The association rules algorithm is a data mining algorithm that is designed for market basket analysis. It defines an item set as a combination of items in a single transaction. The algorithm scans the dataset and counts the number of times item sets appear in transactions.

Answer option C is incorrect. The Decision Trees algorithm is the most popular data mining algorithm, which is used to predict discrete and continuous variables. The reason that this algorithm is so popular is that the results generated are very easy to understand by the user. If a user predicts continuous variables, he gets piecewise multiple linear regression formulae with separate formulae in each node of a tree. The discrete input variables are used by the algorithm to split the tree into nodes. A tree that predicts continuous variables is a Regression Tree.

Answer option D is incorrect. The Naive Bayes algorithm calculates probabilities for each possible state of the input attribute. The user can later use those probabilities to predict an outcome of the target attribute based on the known input attributes. Because this algorithm is quite simple, it builds the models very quickly. Thus, it can be used as a starting point in prediction tasks. This algorithm does not support continuous attributes.

A5.   Answer option A is correct.

The Naive Bayes data mining algorithm is used to calculate the probabilities for each possible state of the input attribute, provided that each state of the predictable attribute is given. These probabilities can be used later to predict an outcome of the target attribute that a user is predicting, based on the known input attributes. This algorithm is very simple and is capable of building the models very quickly. Therefore, this algorithm can be used by users as a starting point in their prediction task. The Naive Bayes algorithm does not support continuous attributes.

Answer option B is incorrect. The Decision Trees algorithm is the most popular data mining algorithm, which is used to predict discrete and continuous variables. The reason that this algorithm is so popular is that the results generated are very easy to understand by the user. If a user predicts continuous variables, he gets piecewise multiple linear regression formulae with separate formulae in each node of a tree. The discrete input variables are used by the algorithm to split the tree into nodes. A tree that predicts continuous variables is a Regression Tree.

Answer option C is incorrect. The Association Rules data mining algorithm is designed for the market basket analysis. The algorithm defines an itemset as a combination of items in a single transaction. The algorithm scans the dataset and counts the number of times the itemsets appear in the transactions. This algorithm should be used for detecting the cross-selling opportunities.

Answer option D is incorrect. The Clustering Algorithm is used to group cases from a dataset into a cluster containing similar characteristics. With the help of these cluster, the users can explore the data and learn about relationships among their cases. Additionally, a user can create predictions from the clustering model created by the algorithm.

Chapter 3 - Designing the BI Architecture

Overview

This chapter describes about the section of how to maintain server health, select a subscription strategy, manage integration services, design a backup strategy, plan and manage upgrades, plan and manage reporting services configuration.

Maintain server health

- Dynamic Management Views (DMVs) are system views that surface the internal counters of the database engine. These views also help the user to present an easily comprehendible dashboard of the database engine performance that can be used to examine the health of a server instance, diagnose problems, etc.

- BIDS (Business Intelligence Development Studio) is a development tool used to create reports, packages, and analysis projects. It is a part of Visual Studio 2005. The tool contains projects and wizards to create the reports, packages and analysis projects either automatically or manually.

Pop Quiz

Q1: What is a development tool used to create reports, packages, and analysis projects?

Ans: BIDS

Q2: What are system views that surface the internal counters of the database engine?

Ans: Dynamic Management Views

Select a subscription strategy.

- A business intelligence solution is used to present data in a variety of ways, such as dashboards, scorecards, and reports. Data visualization is a key aspect of business intelligence and a proper use of these techniques is the best way to make reports in SQL more useful and effective.

- The Report Server temporary database is used by each report server database to store execution data and session, cached reports, and tables that are generated by the report server. By default, the temporary database is named as reportservertempdb. If the temporary database is missing, it is not recreated by the Reporting Services. Although the temporary database does not contain persisted data, it is recommended that a backup copy of the temporary database be taken. This is done mainly to avoid the recreation of the temporary database as part of a failure recovery operation.

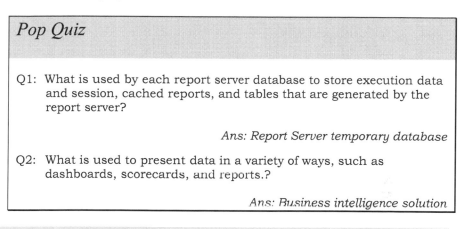

Pop Quiz

Q1: What is used by each report server database to store execution data and session, cached reports, and tables that are generated by the report server?

Ans: Report Server temporary database

Q2: What is used to present data in a variety of ways, such as dashboards, scorecards, and reports.?

Ans: Business intelligence solution

Manage integration services.

- Microsoft SQL Server 2008 provides a scalable enterprise data integration platform with excellent Extract, Transform, Load (ETL), and integration capabilities. These capabilities facilitate organizations to handle data from a wide range of data sources. This data is converted into an Integration Services data type when it enters a data flow in a package. If data has a data type that is not convertible to an Integration Services data type, an error occurs.

- Numeric data is allocated a numeric data type, string data is allocated a character data type, and dates are allocated a date data type. Other data, such as GUIDs and Binary Large Object Blocks (BLOBs), are also allocated suitable Integration Services data types.

<table>
<tr><td>

Pop Quiz

Q1: What is the scope of the sys.dm_exec_query_stats DMV?

Ans: Server

Q2: What action should be taken to allow a user to query DMVs?

Ans: Assign the SELECT permission.

</td></tr>
</table>

Select a subscription strategy

- The snowflake schema is used in the data warehouse applications and is basically an extended StarSchema where each point of the star branches to more points. In the snowflake schema, the star schema dimension tables are more controlled.

- The advantages of the snowflake schema are as follows:

  - Improved query performance due to minimized disk storage for the data.

  - Improved performance by joining smaller normalized tables, rather than large denormalized ones.

- The snowflake schema also increases the flexibility of the application because the normalization lowers the granularity of the dimensions. However, since the snowflake schema has more tables, it also increases the complexities of some of the queries that need to be mapped.

- A business intelligence solution is used to present data in a variety of ways, such as dashboards, scorecards, and reports. Data visualization is a key aspect of business intelligence and a proper use of these techniques is the best way to make reports in SQL more useful and effective.

- The Report Server database is a SQL Server database that stores application state and persistent data. A backup schedule for this database should be created to prevent data loss. The following list describes some of the contents that are stored in the Report Server database:

- Report execution log data

- Subscription and schedule definitions

- Symmetric keys and encrypted connection and credentials for report data sources

- Report snapshots which may include report history and query result

- System-level security settings and system properties

- Items that are managed by the report server and all the security settings and properties that are associated with those items

- The Report Server temporary database is used by each report server database to store execution data and session, cached reports, and tables that are generated by the report server. By default, the temporary database is named as reportservertempdb. If the temporary database is missing, it is not recreated by the Reporting Services. Although the temporary database does not contain persisted data, it is recommended that a backup copy of the temporary database be taken. This is done mainly to avoid the recreation of the temporary database as part of a failure recovery operation.

- The matrix template is used to display aggregated data summaries which are grouped in rows and columns, analogous to a PivotTable or a crosstab

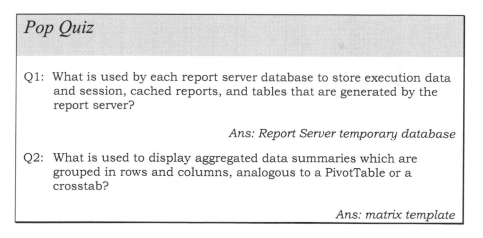

Pop Quiz

Q1: What is used by each report server database to store execution data and session, cached reports, and tables that are generated by the report server?

Ans: Report Server temporary database

Q2: What is used to display aggregated data summaries which are grouped in rows and columns, analogous to a PivotTable or a crosstab?

Ans: matrix template

Manage integration services.

- Microsoft SQL Server 2008 provides a scalable enterprise data integration platform with excellent Extract, Transform, Load (ETL), and integration capabilities. These capabilities facilitate organizations to handle data from a wide range of data sources. This data is converted into an Integration Services data type when it enters a data flow in a package. If data has a data type that is not convertible to an Integration Services data type, an error occurs.

- Numeric data is allocated a numeric data type, string data is allocated a character data type, and dates are allocated a date data type. Other data, such as GUIDs and Binary Large Object Blocks (BLOBs), are also allocated suitable Integration Services data types.

- Spatial data types were introduced in SQL Server 2008 to store spatial information. These are of two types as follows:

  - Geometry data type

  - Geography data type

- SSIS (SQL Server Integration Services) is an upgrade of DTS (Data Transformation Services), which is a feature of the previous version of SQL Server. SSIS packages can be created in BIDS (Business Intelligence Development Studio). These can be used to merge data from heterogeneous data sources into SQL Server. They can also be used to populate data warehouses, to clean and standardize data, and to automate administrative tasks.

- The Business Intelligence Development Studio, the 32-bit development environment for Integration Services packages, is not supported on the Itanium 64-bit operating system and is not installed on Itanium servers.

- The Package Migration Wizard can be started with the help of either Business Intelligence Development Studio (BIDS) or SQL Server Management Studio (SSMS).

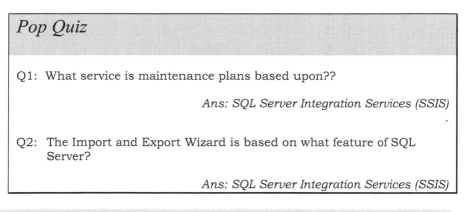

Q1: What service is maintenance plans based upon??

Ans: SQL Server Integration Services (SSIS)

Q2: The Import and Export Wizard is based on what feature of SQL Server?

Ans: SQL Server Integration Services (SSIS)

Design a backup strategy

- Backing up a database is a process of keeping a duplicate copy of a database to another location. The database is backed up due to the following reasons:

  - If a database is corrupted, the backup copy can be used in its place.

  - If a database object or a record is changed by mistake, the object or the record can be copied back from the backup to the current database.

- The full recovery model makes use of log backups to avoid data loss in the broadest range of failure events. In this case, backing and restoring the log backups is needed. The benefit of using log backups is that the database can be restored to any point of time that is contained within a log backup. Log backups can be used in a sequence to roll a database forward to any point of time that is contained in one of the transaction logs.

- A partial backup is designed to be used under the simple recovery model to improve flexibility for backing up very large databases, which consist of one or more read-only file groups. A partial backup resembles a full database backup. It contains all the data in the primary file group, every read/write file group, and read-only files that are specified optionally. A partial backup is useful whenever read-only file groups are needed to be excluded.

- The Database Engine is the underlined component of a database. It is a collection of information stored on the computer in a systematic way. It is mainly used for storing, securing, and processing data in the database. The Database Engine ensures controlled access and rapid transaction processing to meet the requirements of the most demanding data consuming applications in any organization. SQL Server supports up to fifty instances of the Database Engine on one computer.

- Backup utility is used to take backup of the database, transaction log files, or one or more files or filegroups. Backup utility supports two modes of backup as described below:

- The full backup backs up all the selected files for backup and takes maximum space and time to backup. To restore data, you should restore the last full backup tape.

- The differential backup is faster than the full backup. The differential backup backs up only those files that have been created, or have changed since the last backup. To restore data, you should first restore the last full backup tape and then last differential backup tapes.

Pop Quiz

Q1: Which object that can be processed in SSAS stores data?

Ans: dimensions

Q2: Which SSAS storage mode is used to store metadata and source data?

Ans: Multidimensional Online Analytical Processing (MOLAP)

Plan and manage upgrades

- The Parallel processing setting is used for batch processing. This setting causes Analysis Services to fork off processing tasks to execute in parallel inside a single transaction. If a failure occurs, the result generated is a rollback of all changes. A user can set the maximum number of parallel tasks, or allow the server to decide the optimal distribution. The Parallel processing option is useful for speeding up the processing.

- SQL Server 2008 Upgrade Advisor helps a user to prepare for upgrades to SQL Server 2008. It generates reports after analyzing the previously installed SQL Server 2005, SQL Server 2000, or SQL Server 7.0. On the basis of the report generated, the issues that have to be fixed are identified either before or after the upgrade to SQL Server 2008. The

Upgrade Advisor Home page appears when Upgrade Advisor is run. The tools that could be run from the home page are as follows:

- Upgrade Advisor Analysis Wizard

- Upgrade Advisor Report Viewer

- Upgrade Advisor Help

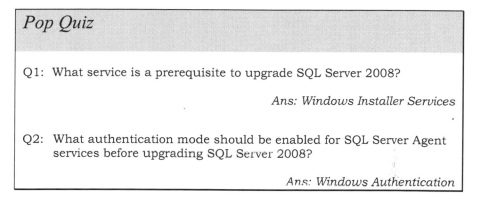

Pop Quiz

Q1: What service is a prerequisite to upgrade SQL Server 2008?

Ans: Windows Installer Services

Q2: What authentication mode should be enabled for SQL Server Agent services before upgrading SQL Server 2008?

Ans: Windows Authentication

Plan and manage reporting services configuration

- A Database Mail profile is an ordered collection of related Database Mail accounts. In order to send mail, a user must be a member of the DatabaseMailUserRole in the msdb database, and should have access to at least one Database Mail profile. Profiles permit database administrators to reconfigure stored procedures and database applications that use e-mail without changing the application code. For example, a profile can be configured with one set of e-mail accounts during application development and testing, and then be updated with another set of accounts when the application shifts to production. The application uses the same profile name, but sends e-mail using a different list of e-mail servers.

- The sp_send_dbmail stored procedure is used to send an e-mail message to the specified recipients. The message may include file attachments, a query result set, or both. It returns the mailitem_id of the message when the mail is successfully placed in the Database Mail queue. This stored procedure is in the msdb database. The execute permissions for sp_send_dbmail default to all members of the DatabaseMailUser database role in the msdb database.

- The Reporting Services Configuration Manager tool performs the following common setup and configuration tasks that are required to implement an SSRS instance:

  - Defining the ASP.NET account

  - Creation of the virtual directories

  - Configuration of the Service Startup account

  - Management of the symmetric encryption keys

  - Setting up the database connection to the SSRS repository

  - Defining operational accounts for e-mail and other administration tasks

  - Performing initialization steps to enable new instances for a scale-out deployment

- The Reporting Services Configuration tool is used to configure a Reporting Services installation. If a report server is installed by using the files-only installation option, this tool should be used to configure the server before it is used. If the default configuration installation option is used to install a report server, this tool can be used to modify or verify the settings that were specified during the setup. Reporting Services Configuration can be used to configure a remote or local server instance.

- The SQL Server Configuration Manager is a tool used to manage the services associated with SQL Server. It can be used to configure network connections, network protocols, and network libraries. The SQL Server Configuration Manager is a Microsoft Management Console snap-in that is available from the Start menu. It uses Windows Management Instrumentation (WMI) to view and change some server settings.

- A configuration is a set of property-value pairs that are used to define the properties of the package and its containers, tasks, variables, event-handlers, and connections when the package executes. It is possible to update properties without modifying the package by using configurations.

- When the package is executed, the configuration information is loaded as a result of which the values of properties get updated. For example, the connection string of connection can be updated with the help of a configuration. When the package is installed on a different computer, the configuration is saved and then deployed with the package. To support the package in a different environment, the values in the configuration can be updated when the package is installed.

- Database Mail is used for sending e-mail messages from the Microsoft SQL Server 2005 and 2008 Database Engine. It can be used by database applications to send e-mail messages to users. The messages may include results of the query, and can also contain files from any resource on the user's network. Database Mail is designed for reliability, scalability, security, and supportability. It provides a robust, high-performance replacement for the most commonly requested features of SQL Mail. Database Mail is designed to function with SMTP servers.

- SQL Server Surface Area Configuration is a tool that is used to enable, disable, start, or stop the features, services, and remote connectivity of SQL Server 2005 and 2008 installations. This tool can be used on local and remote servers. Windows Management Instrumentation (WMI) is used by SQL Server Surface Area Configuration to view and change server settings.

- The Database Mail XPs option of the sp_configure system stored procedure is used to enable Database Mail on the server. It has the following two possible values:

  - 1 indicating that the Database Mail is available.

  - 0 indicating that the Database Mail is not available. This is the default value.

  The setting takes effect immediately without a server stop and restart.

- Database Mail can be enabled using either the sp_configure stored procedure or the Database Mail Configuration Wizard. Additionally, the Database Mail Configuration Wizard can be used to create a Database Mail profile. Once it is enabled and a profile has been created, the sp_send_dbmail stored procedure can be used to send emails.

- Reporting Services Configuration Manager can enable and name the virtual directories for the report server and Report Manager after the installation.

- A configuration is a set of property-value pairs that defines the properties of the package and its tasks, containers, variables, connections, and event handlers when the package runs.

- The Build package verification option is used to specify the sequential Build number associated with the build.

- The Reporting Services Configuration Manager tool can be used to change or create the virtual directories for the report server and Report Manager after installation.

Pop Quiz

Q1: What tool is available in Business Intelligence Development Studio?

Ans: Report Designer and Model Designer

.

Q2: Which is NOT an SSRS command-line utility?

Ans: RSUtil.exe

Test Your Knowledge

Q1. Peter works as an Administrator for Infotech Inc. The company has a SQL Server 2008 computer. Over the weekend, the company experienced a system failure, but now everything appears to be coming back to normal without any major issue. However, users now complain that they are seeing strange values in some of the queries they run against the database that was upgraded from SQL Server 2005. It looks as if some of the columns now contain larger numbers than expected. Which of the following clauses of the DBCC CHECKDB statement should Peter use to resolve the issue?

    A.   DATA_PURITY

    B.   PHYSICAL_ONLY

    C.   ALL_ERRORMSGS

    D.   REPAIR_REBUILD

Q2. You manage a SQL Server 2008 server within a domain named uCertify.com. You want to configure the SQL Server 2008 server to send email messages to users in the domain. What should you do?

    A.   Enable SQLMail using sp_configure and create a MAPI profile.

    B.   Configure SQLMail to use the sp_send_dbmail stored procedure.

    C.   Enable Database Mail using the Database Mail Configuration Wizard and create a MAPI profile.

    D.   Enable Database Mail using sp_configure and create a Database Mail profile.

Q3. You work as an Administrator for Bluewell Inc. The company has a SQL Server 2008 computer. You have installed the SQL Server 2008 Reporting Services (SSRS) instance. You want to create the virtual directories for the report server and Report Manager after installation. Which of the following should you use to accomplish the task?

    A.   Reporting Services Configuration Manager

    B.   SQL Server Configuration Manager

C.   dta utility

D.   SQL Server Profiler

Q4. Which of the following objects of a package is a set of property-value pairs that defines the properties of the package and its tasks, containers, variables, connections, and event handlers when the package runs?

A.   Configuration

B.   Log providers

C.   Variables

D.   Event handlers

Q5. Which of the following tools can be used to change or create the virtual directories for the report server and Report Manager after installation?

A.   Query Designer tool

B.   Reporting Services Configuration Manager tool

C.   Report Builder tool

D.   Report Manager tool

Answer Explanation

A1.   Answer option A is correct.

Peter should use the DATA_PURITY clause of the DBCC CHECKDB statement to accomplish the task. The DATA_PURITY clause of the DBCC CHECKDB statement is used to check the database for column values that are out-of-range or invalid. For example, DBCC CHECKDB detects columns with date and time values that are larger than or less than the acceptable range for the datetime data type; or decimal or approximate-numeric data type columns with precision values that are invalid. This is useful only for databases that have been upgraded from earlier versions of SQL Server because databases created in SQL Server 2005 and later versions have column-value integrity checks enabled by default.

Answer option B is incorrect. The PHYSICAL_ONLY clause of the DBCC CHECKDB statement permits the DBCC CHECKDB statement to check only the physical structure of the database file. It checks only the structure of the page and record headers, the physical structure of B-trees, and the allocation consistency of the database. It can also detect torn pages, checksum failures, and common hardware failures that can compromise a user's data. The PHYSICAL_ONLY clause causes a much shorter run-time for DBCC CHECKDB on large databases when compared to the DBCC CHECKDB statement being run without it. Thus, this clause is recommended for frequent use on production systems.

Answer option C is incorrect. The ALL_ERRORMSGS clause of the DBCC CHECKDB statement displays all reported errors for each object. In SQL Server 2008 Service Pack 1, all error messages are displayed by default. Specifying or omitting this option has no effect. In earlier versions of SQL Server, with the exception of SQL Server 2005 SP3, only the first 200 error messages for each object are displayed if ALL_ERRORMSGS is not specified. Error messages are sorted by object ID, except for those messages generated from the tempdb database.

Answer option D is incorrect. The REPAIR_REBUILD clause of the DBCC CHECKDB statement performs repairs that have no possibility of data loss. This includes fast repairs, such as repairing missing rows in non-clustered indexes, and extra time-consuming repairs, such as rebuilding an index. It does not repair errors involving FILESTREAM data.

A2.   Answer option D is correct.

Database Mail can be enabled using either the sp_configure stored procedure or the Database Mail Configuration Wizard. Additionally, the Database Mail Configuration Wizard can be used to create a Database Mail profile. Once it is enabled and a profile has been created, the sp_send_dbmail stored procedure can be used to send emails.

The Database mail Configuration Wizard can be accessed via the SQL Server Management Studio (SSMS) in the Management node. Right-click Database Mail and select Configure Database Mail. This wizard allows you to configure multiple profiles, which can be used to send email using different SMTP servers.

Answer option A is incorrect. SQL Mail provides a way to receive e-mail messages generated by SQL Server. These messages can be triggered to provide the status of a job or a warning caused by an alert. SQL Mail can include a result set in reply to e-mail messages that contain queries. SQL Mail allows SQL Server to send and receive e-mails by establishing a client connection with a mail server. SQL Server uses two services to handle mail, MSSQLServer and SQLAgentMail.SQL Mail is considered deprecated. Database Mail should be used instead. While SQL Mail needed a MAPI profile, Database Mail does not use MAPI profiles.

Answer option B is incorrect. SQL Mail is considered deprecated. Database Mail should be used instead. Once Database Mail is configured, the sp_send_dbmail stored procedure can be used.

Answer option C is incorrect. Database Mail does not use MAPI profiles. Previous editions of SQL Server used MAPI profiles, but Database Mail instead is configured to send email directly to SMTP servers.

A3. Answer option A is correct.

The Reporting Services Configuration Manager tool performs the following common setup and configuration tasks that are required to implement an SSRS instance:

- Defining the ASP.NET account

- Creation of the virtual directories

- Configuration of the Service Startup account

- Management of the symmetric encryption keys

- Setting up the database connection to the SSRS repository

- Defining operational accounts for e-mail and other administration tasks

- Performing initialization steps to enable new instances for a scale-out deployment

Answer option B is incorrect. The SQL Server Configuration Manager is a tool used to manage the services associated with SQL Server. It can be used to configure network connections, network protocols, and network libraries. The SQL Server Configuration Manager is a Microsoft Management Console snap-in that is available from the Start menu. It uses Windows Management Instrumentation (WMI) to view and change some server settings.

Answer option C is incorrect. The dta utility is the command prompt edition of Database Engine Tuning Advisor. The dta utility allows users to use Database Engine Tuning Advisor functionality in applications and scripts.

The dta utility analyzes a workload and suggests physical design structures to enhance server performance for that workload. The workload can be a SQL Server Profiler trace file or a table, or a Transact-SQL script. Physical design structures comprise indexes, indexed views, and partitioning. After examining a workload, the dta utility produces a suggestion for the physical design of databases and can produce the necessary script to implement the suggestion.

Answer option D is incorrect. SQL Server Profiler is a tool used to monitor and trace events. The events generated can be used to find the slow running queries and to determine the cause of a deadlock and that of slow running queries. The events that are captured by SQL Server Profiler are as follows:

- Login connections, failures, and disconnections

- Transact-SQL statements

- Remote procedure call

- The start or end of a stored procedure and statements within it

- The start or end of a transact-SQL batch

- An error written to the SQL Server error log

- Locks and deadlocks

A4.   Answer option A is correct.

A configuration is a set of property-value pairs that are used to define the properties of the package and its containers, tasks, variables, event-handlers, and connections when the package executes. It is possible to update properties without modifying the package by using configurations.

When the package is executed, the configuration information is loaded as a result of which the values of properties get updated. For example, the connection string of connection can be updated with the help of a configuration. When the package is installed on a different computer, the configuration is saved and then deployed with the package. To support the package in a different environment, the values in the configuration can be updated when the package is installed.

Answer option B is incorrect. Log providers are included in SQL Server Integration Services, which can be used to implement logging in packages, tasks, and containers. It is possible to capture run-time information with the help of logging. This helps a user to audit and troubleshoot a package every time it is executed. For example, with the help of a log, it is possible to capture the name of the operator who ran the package and the time the package began and finished. When a log is added to a package, the log provider and location of the log is chosen. The format for the log data is specified by the log provider.

Answer option C is incorrect. Variables are used to store values that a SQL Server Integration Services package and its containers, event handlers, and tasks can use at runtime. Variables can also be used by the scripts in the Script task and the Script component. The precedence constraints that sequence containers and tasks into a workflow can use variables when their constraint definitions include expressions.

Answer option D is incorrect. Event handlers enable SQL Server Integration Services (SSIS) packages to respond programmatically to events that are raised at run time by tasks and containers. This is the new feature found in SQL server 2005/2008 that can enhance the manageability of SSIS.

At run time, events are fired by package executables like tasks, packages and containers to signal a number of different states including: error conditions, when a task completes, when a task has started, or a change in variable status. The functionality of the package can be extended by taking advantage of SSIS's ability to add custom event handlers for different package elements. The SSIS

Designer's Event Handler tab, found in the Business Intelligence Development Studio (BIDS), is used to create event handlers.

A5.   Answer option B is correct.

The Reporting Services Configuration Manager tool can be used to change or create the virtual directories for the report server and Report Manager after installation.The SQL Server Configuration Manager is a tool used to manage the services associated with SQL Server. It can be used to configure network connections, network protocols, and network libraries. The SQL Server Configuration Manager is a Microsoft Management Console snap-in that is available from the Start menu. It uses Windows Management Instrumentation (WMI) to view and change some server settings.

Answer option A is incorrect. The Report Model query designer is used to modify or create queries that run against a report model that has been published to a report server. Clickthrough data exploration is supported by the reports that run against models. The path of data exploration is determined by the query at run time. In order to use the Report Model query designer, data source that points to a published model should be defined. The Report Model query designer can be used in either graphical or generic mode.

Answer option C is incorrect. Report Builder in SQL Server Reporting Services (SSRS) 2008 is a totally new tool as compared to Report Builder in SSRS 2005. Report Builder 1.0 in SSRS 2005 is a restricted tool, available from Report Manager, which is generally used by business users to create reports based on report models that are already created. Report Builder 2.0 in SSRS 2008 is an entirely new, stand-alone authoring tool analogous to Microsoft Office applications that can take advantage of all of the features of SSRS. It is not included with SQL Server 2008 release-to-manufacturing (RTM). However, Report Builder 1.0 is still part of the product.

Answer option D is incorrect. Report Manager is a Web-based report access and management tool that can be used to administer a single report server instance from a remote location over an HTTP connection. Report Manager can also be used for its report viewer and navigation features.

Chapter 4 - Designing the BI Architecture

Overview

This chapter describes about the section of how to design integration between data visualization components, design the data warehouse, plan for scalability, plan for performance, manage team development issues, design a security strategy, and plan the configuration of a primary data source.

Design integration between data visualization components.

- SharePoint integrated mode enables the integration of Reporting Services with the SharePoint databases and security model. These features become available when a user configures a report server to run within a larger deployment of a SharePoint 3.0 product or technology. This mode requires additional software and configuration. It also necessitates that a report server instance be dedicated for integrated operations. The benefit of doing this is a rich level of integration that allows a user to access and manage report server content types using the application pages and data stores of a SharePoint Web application.

- The SQL Server Reporting Services (SSRS) is a server-based reporting platform that can be used to create and manage tabular, graphical, matrix, and free-form reports that contain data from multidimensional and relational data sources. The report that is created can be viewed and managed over a World Wide Web-based connection.

- The geometry data type is a type of spatial data type which is used to store planar (flat-earth) data in SQL Server 2008. It is generally used to store XY coordinates that represent points, lines, and polygons in a two-dimensional space.

- The geometry data type supports a flat 2D surface with XY coordinates for representing points. Points can be on lines and can also mark the edges of polygons. There are methods like STintersects, STarea, STDistance, STTouch, etc. which assist the geometry data type. For example, storing XY coordinates in the geometry data type can be used to map the exterior of a building.

- Filestream is not a data type, but is a variant of the VARBINARY(MAX) data type which enables unstructured data to be stored in the file system instead of being stored in the SQL Server database.

- The geography data type stores ellipsoidal (round-earth) data. It deals with latitude and longitude coordinates representing points, lines, and polygons on the earth's surface. This data type is used to store geodetic spatial data and perform operations on it. For example, GPS data that represents the lay of a land is one example of data that can be stored in the geography data type.

- The hierarchyid data type is used to enable database applications to model hierarchical tree structures, such as the organization chart of a business. It is designed to store values that represent the position of nodes of a hierarchal tree structure. For example, the hierarchyid data type makes it simple to represent these types of relationships without the need of multiple parent/child tables and complex joins.

- As compared to the standard data types, the hierarchyid data type is a CLR user-defined type providing various methods to manipulate the date stored within it. The hierarchyid data type is used to store hierarchical data; it does not automatically represent a hierarchical structure. A hierarchyid data type can be considered as a place to store positional nodes of a tree structure, not as a way to create the tree structure.

Pop Quiz

Q1: Which is used to design and implement OnLine Analytical Processing (OLAP) cubes and data mining models to support Business Intelligence (BI) solutions?

Ans: SQL Server Reporting Services (SSRS)

Q2: Which can be best used to deliver dynamic reports?

Ans: SQL Server Analysis Services (SSAS)

Design the data warehouse.

- The MERGE statement in Transact-SQL carries out insert, update, or delete operations on a target table. For example, the user can synchronize two tables by inserting, updating, or deleting rows in one table based on differences found in the other table.

- MOLAP (Multidimensional Online Analytical Processing) is the default storage mode for dimensions. The dimension that uses MOLAP stores its data in a multidimensional structure in the instance of Microsoft's SQL

Server Analysis Services. This MOLAP is created and populated when the dimension is processed. The quality performance of MOLAP dimensions is better than ROLAP (Relational Online Analytical Processing) dimensions.

- ROLAP (Relational Online Analytical Processing) is the storage mode for the dimensions. The dimensions that uses ROLAP store the data in the tables that are used to define dimension. The ROLAP storage mode, at the expense of query performance, can support large dimensions without duplicating large amount of data. The ROLAP storage mode can also support real-time OLAP because the dimension relies directly on the tables in the data source view that is used to define the dimensions.

- HOLAP (Hybrid Online Analytical Processing) is a compromise between MOLAP (Multidimensional Online Analytical Processing) and ROLAP (Relational Online Analytical Processing). The storage of aggregates is done in the MOLAP file, while the base-level detail is kept in the data mart. This enhances the performance while browsing aggregates, but it slows down when a user "drills down" to base-level detail.

- In Low Latency MOLAP, detail data and aggregations are stored in multidimensional format. While MOLAP objects are reprocessed in a cache, the server listens for notifications of changes to the data and switches to real-time ROLAP. A silence interval of around 10 seconds is required before the cache is updated. If the silence interval is not attained, there is an override interval of 10 minutes. As data changes, processing occurs automatically with a target latency of 30 minutes after the first change.

- This setting is usually used for a data source that has frequent updates and when query performance is more important than always providing the most current data. This setting processes MOLAP objects automatically whenever required after the latency interval. Performance is slower while the MOLAP objects are being reprocessed.

- In Medium Latency MOLAP, detail data and aggregations are stored in multidimensional format. While MOLAP objects are reprocessed in a cache, the server listens for notifications of changes to the data and switches to real-time ROLAP. A silence interval of around 10 seconds is required before the cache is updated. If the silence interval is not attained, there is an override interval of 10 minutes. As data changes, processing occurs automatically with a target latency of four hours.

- This setting is usually used for a data source that has frequent or less frequent updates and when query performance is more important than always providing the most current data. This setting processes MOLAP objects automatically whenever required after the latency interval. Performance is slower while the MOLAP objects are being reprocessed.

- In Automatic MOLAP, detail data and aggregations are stored in multidimensional format. The server listens for notifications and retains the current MOLAP cache while it builds a new one. The server never switches to real-time OLAP, and while the new cache is built, the queries may be stale. A silence interval of around 10 seconds is required before the creation of a new MOLAP cache. If the silence interval is not attained, there is an override interval of 10 minutes. Processing occurs automatically as data changes with a target latency of two hours.

- This setting is typically used for a data source when the performance of the query is of prime importance. MOLAP objects are processed automatically by this setting, whenever required, after the latency interval. The most recent data is not returned by the queries while the new cache is being built and processed.

- In Scheduled MOLAP, detail data and aggregations are stored in a multidimensional format. Notification is not received by the server when the data changes, and processing automatically occurs every 24 hours. This setting is normally used for a data source when there is requirement of only daily updates. In the MOLAP cache, queries are always against data that is not discarded until a new cache is built and its objects are processed.

- Online analytical processing, or OLAP, is an approach to quickly answer multi-dimensional analytical queries. OLAP is part of the broader category of business intelligence, which also encompasses relational reporting and data mining. The typical applications of OLAP are in business reporting for sales, marketing, management reporting, business process management (BPM), budgeting and forecasting, financial reporting, and similar areas.

- Databases configured for OLAP use a multidimensional data model, allowing for complex analytical and ad-hoc queries with a rapid execution time. They borrow aspects of navigational databases and hierarchical databases that are faster than relational databases.

- The output of an OLAP query is typically displayed in a matrix (or pivot) format. The dimensions form the rows and columns of the matrix; the measures form the values.

- The Index Tuning Wizard suggests an optimal set of indexes for a database based on the workload file. A workload file can include SQL scripts or a SQL Profiler trace. The Index Tuning Wizard analyzes the workload and recommends an index configuration that will improve the performance of the database. It can be used to match the recommendation with the existing set of indexes to determine whether the useful indexes have been created.

Pop Quiz

Q1: Which type of data mart can be used to unite an organization's data in one data warehouse?

Ans: The transformation process is performed locally in the operational environment and then loaded to the warehouse.

Q2: Which is NOT a Business Intelligence environment layer?

Ans: The application layer

Manage team development issues.

- The syntax of a default Report Manager URL for a named instance of Reporting Services is http://[ComputerName]/Reports_[InstanceName].

- Database Engine Tuning Advisor is a tool that tunes a database for better query performance by analyzing a workload that is a set of T-SQL statements. It suggests clustered indexes, nonclustered indexes, indexed views, and partitioning. Database Engine Tuning Advisor in SQL Server 2005 replaces the Index Tuning Wizard of SQL Server 2000. This tool provides two user interfaces: a graphical user interface (GUI) and the dta command prompt utility.

Pop Quiz

Q1: Which architecture is used as the core of integration services in SQL Server 2008?

Ans: Buffer-oriented architecture

Q2: Which report can be built using the BI feature of SQL Server 2008?

Ans: Ad hoc report

Plan the configuration of a primary data source.

- A Shared data source is a set of data source connection properties that are referenced by multiple reports, models, and data-driven subscriptions. Shared data sources provide a simple way for managing data source properties that change from time to time. If a user account or password changes, or if one moves the database to a different server, he can update the connection information in one place.

- Before updating an instance of Analysis Services, you should back up the following:

  - Analysis Services databases

  - Analysis Services configuration file

  - The dataset contains three elements; data source, command type, and query string.

- Change data capture (CDC) is used to keep a record of the insert, update, and delete operations applied to a table in the SQL Server database.

Pop Quiz

Q1: Which storage mode is used to store both data and aggregations in a file-based multidimensional structure created and managed by the SSAS server??

Ans: MULTIDIMENSIONAL OLAP

Q2: Which processing option of OLAP deletes the partition data and applies Process Default to the cube dimensions?

Ans: Process Structure

Design a security strategy.

- The RSPreviewPolicy.config XML Configuration file of SSRS contains security policies for the server extensions.

- A linked measure group allows a user to share data across cubes within duplicating data.

Pop Quiz

Q1: What contains security policies for the server extensions?

Ans: RSPreviewPolicy.config XML Configuration file

Q2: Which allows a user to share data across cubes within duplicating data?

Ans: linked measure group

Test Your Knowledge

Q1.   You work as an Administrator for Bluewell Inc. The company has a SQL Server 2008 computer. You are managing a SQL Server 2008 Analysis Services instance. You want to update an instance of the Analysis Service, but before updating it, what should you back up?

Each correct answer represents a complete solution. Choose all that apply.

A.   Analysis Services databases

B.   Analysis Services configuration file

C.   Analysis Services repository

D.   Analysis Services Server

Q2.   What are the elements of a dataset?

Each correct answer represents a complete solution. Choose all that apply.

A.   Data source

B.   Command type

C.   Query string

D.   Query structure

Q3.   You work as a Network Administrator for uCertify Inc. The company uses SQL Server 2008 as the database application. There is a database named Sales. A task has been assigned to you to track the details of the inserts, updates, and deletes which are applied to the tables in the Sales database. The entries corresponding to those changes are added to a database log. This makes the details of the changes available in an easy-to-use format.

What will you do to accomplish the task?

Each correct answer represents a part of the solution. Choose all that apply.

A.   Update the tables and keep a record of the changes manually.

B.   Use the change data capture feature in SQL Server 2008.

C.   Use SQL dependencies to track the changes.

D.   Use the sys.sp_cdc_enable_table procedure to identify the source table as tracked table.

Q4. You work as an Administrator for TechMart Inc. The company has a SQL Server 2008 computer that contains a database named Employees. You manage SQL Server 2008 Analysis Services (SSAS) for the company. The Employees database contains a measure group in a cube. You develop a new database called Department. You want to incorporate the same measure group that was developed for the Employees database in the cube that was developed for the Department database. What should you do?

A.   Create a linked measure group.

B.   Create a linked dimension.

C.   Create a linked server configuration.

D.   Create a new measure group in the Department database.

Q5. Which of the following XML Configuration files of SQL Server 2008 Reporting Services (SSRS) contains security policies for the server extensions?

A.   RSPreviewPolicy.config

B.   Web.config

C.   RSReportServer.config

D.   RSMgrPolicy.config

Answer Explanation

A1. Answer options A and B are correct.

Before updating an instance of Analysis Services, you should back up the following:

- Analysis Services databases: By default, these are installed to C:\Program Files\Microsoft SQL Server\MSAS10\\OLAP\Data\.

- Analysis Services configuration file: It is the Analysis Services configuration setting in the msmdsrv.ini configuration file. By default, this is located in the C:\Program Files\Microsoft SQL

- Server\MSAS10\\OLAP\Config\ directory.

Answer option C is incorrect. Analysis Services repository is the database that contains the Analysis Services repository. This step is required only if Analysis Services was configured to work with the Decision Support Objects (DSO) library.

Answer option D is incorrect. There is no need to take a backup of the Analysis Services Server.

A2. Answer options A, B, and C are correct.

Following are the three main elements of a dataset:

- Data source: A data source configures the driver and connection properties to connect to the data.

- Command type: The command type can be a text or stored procedure.

- Query string: Text commands use the query language/string of the data provider, as an example Transact-SQL is used for the relational engine, and DMX or MDX is used for Analysis services.

Answer option D is incorrect. Query structure is not an element of the data set.

A3. Answer options B and D are correct.

Change data capture (CDC) is used to keep a record of the insert, update, and delete operations applied to a table in the SQL Server database. This makes the details of the changes available in an easy-to-use format.

The transaction log serves as input to CDC. As the inserts, updates, and deletes are applied to the source tables, the entries describing those changes are added to the log. The filtered result set is generally used by an application process to update the source representation in an external environment.

Answer option A is incorrect. Keeping the record of the changes manually cannot accomplish the task in case of a large database.

Answer option C is incorrect. SQL dependencies are used to make one entity dependent on another entity. These are the named references used in SQL expressions. The entity that refers to another entity in its definition is called the referencing entity and the entity that is referred to by another entity is called the referenced entity.

For example, views and stored procedures depend upon the existence of tables that contain the data returned by the view or procedure. There are two types of dependencies tracked by the Database Engine, which are as follows:

- Schema-bound dependency

- Non-schema-bound dependency

A4. Answer option A is correct.

As mentioned in the scenario, the Employee database contains a cube with a measure group that you want to incorporate in the Department database. To accomplish this task, you should create a linked measure group that allows you to share data across cubes within duplicating data. The linked measure group allows a user to share data across cubes within duplicating data. A cube in Microsoft SQL Server Analysis Services is based on a data source view. With some usage limitations, the linked measure groups are treated like any other measure group in a cube. When accessed by client applications, the linked measure groups are identical to other measure groups. These linked measure groups are also queried in the same manner as the other measure groups.

Answer option B is incorrect. A linked dimension in Microsoft SQL Server Analysis Services (SSAS) is based on dimension that is stored in another database of the Analysis Services. The source database for a linked dimension can be on a different server or on the same server. With the help of a linked dimension it is possible to create, maintain, and store a dimension on one Analysis Service database, and also make that dimension available to users of multiple databases. To users, a linked dimension appears like any other dimension.

Answer option C is incorrect. A linked server configuration is used to enable the SQL Server so that it may execute commands against OLE DB data source on the remote servers. Following advantages are offered by the linked servers:

- The ability to access the remote server

- The ability to address diverse data sources similarly

- The ability to issue distributed queries, commands, updates, and transactions on the heterogeneous data sources across the enterprise

Answer option D is incorrect. The Department database requires the same measure group that is present in the Employee database; therefore, creating the same measure group again will increase the administrative effort. Instead, the same task can be accomplished by creating a linked measure group. A measure group is a collection of measures. A measure is a fact, which is a measurement or a transactional value that a user may want to aggregate. When measures are sourced from columns in one or more source tables, they form a group called measure group. A cube is a set of related measures and dimensions that is used to analyze data.

A5.   Answer option A is correct.

The different XML configuration files to handle advanced service settings, user defaults, and policy managements are described in the following table:

File	Description
RSSrvPolicy.config	It is used to store the policy settings for the report Server Web service.
RSReportServer.co	It is the primary configuration file

nfig	that contains settings for the Report Server Web part and Report Manager.
RSMgrPolicy.config	It contains policy settings for the Report Manager application.
Web.config	This file contains ASP.NET settings for the Report Manager and Report Server.
RSReportDesigner. config	This file contains configuration settings such as rendering devices for the Report Designer application.
RSPreviewPolicy.co nfig	This file contains the security policy for the server extensions.
ReportingServices Services.exe.config	This file contains trace and logging settings for the Report Service service.

Chapter 5 - Resourcing Project Plans

Overview

This chapter describes about the section of how to design control flow, design data flow, plan the deployment of SSIS packages, design the configuration file for an SSIS package, and design a logging and auditing strategy.

Design control flow.

- Maintenance plans are used to create a workflow of the tasks to make sure that the database is optimized, is free of inconsistencies, and is regularly backed up. In SQL Server Database Engine, maintenance plans create an Integration Services package, which is run by a SQL Server Agent job. These maintenance tasks can be run at scheduled intervals either manually or automatically.

- An SSIS package is a collection of connections, control flow elements, data flow elements, event handlers, variables, and configurations. It can be used to perform various tasks, such as importing or exporting a database or database objects, backing up or restoring databases, etc. The package can be either used in a graphical tool or can be used programmatically. The package is either saved in the MSDB system database or to a file system.

- An FTP connection manager allows a package to make a connection to a File Transfer Protocol (FTP) server. The FTP task included in SQL Server Integration Services makes use of this connection manager.

- When an FTP connection manager is added to a package, Integration Services creates a connection manager that can be resolved as an FTP connection at run time, sets the connection manager properties, and adds the connection manager to the Connections collection on the package.

- The Fuzzy Grouping transformation is used to perform data cleaning tasks by recognizing rows of data that are expected to be duplicates and selecting a canonical row of data to use in standardizing the data. A connection to an instance of SQL Server is required by the Fuzzy Grouping transformation to create temporary SQL Server tables that the transformation algorithm requires to do its work. Two features included in the Fuzzy Grouping transformation for customizing the grouping it performs are token delimiters and similarity threshold.

- The ActiveX Script task is used to run Microsoft Visual Basic Scripting Edition (VBScript) and JavaScript code. It is also included chiefly for legacy support when a Data Transformation Services (DTS) package is migrated to SQL Server Integration Services (SSIS).

- The Data Mining Query task performs data mining queries and allows a user to capture the results for analysis. The Data Mining Query task according to Analysis Services data mining models is built to run prediction queries. This task is similar to the Analysis Services Execute DDL task in which the user can execute subsequent mining queries against a processed mining model in Analysis Server.

- The Maintenance Cleanup task can be used to perform the removal operation of older files like maintenance plan execution reports, database backup files, etc. The user can use this task when creating maintenance plans, as it removes old files which are no longer required by the user.

Pop Quiz

Q1: Which tab in an SSIS package will you use to open and configure SSIS logs?

Ans: Control Flow

Q2: Which procedure is used to issue operating system commands directly to the Windows command shell via T-SQL code?

Ans: xp_cmdshell

Design data flow

- The Data Flow task is used to encapsulate the data flow engine that moves data between sources and destinations. It allows a user to clean, modify, and transform data as it is moved. Addition of a Data Flow task to a package control flow makes it possible for the package to transform, extract, and load data.

- At least one data flow component is present in a data flow, but it is usually a set of connected data flow components: sources that extract data; transformations that route, modify, or summarize data; and destinations that load data. Paths are used to connect components in the data flow.

- The Data Flow task, at run time, builds an execution plan from the data flow. The plan is executed by the data flow engine. It is possible to create a Data Flow task without having a data flow, but the task executes only if it includes at least one data flow. Multiple data flows can be included in the Data Flow task.

- The lookup in no caching mode executes one query for each row in the pipeline against the reference data source. At the same time, it always performs the lookup against the most up-to-date value in the reference data and provides the least performance. In data warehousing, lookups are used to retrieve surrogate keys from large dimensions using source keys. During this process, the latency is unlikely to be issued and users are more concerned with the performance.

- The lookup in Partial Caching mode searches the cache for a query match. If a match is not found, then a query against the data source will be executed and the pipeline row is redirected as configured. If a match is found, it is held in the cache.

- The lookup in Full Caching mode loads the cache from the data source and holds it in memory for the lookup process during the pre-execution phase. The idea behind this is that the disk read operation is performed once and that the data is cached in memory. Thus, the cached data stored in the memory for additional lookups can be re-used. This is the default mode used by the lookup.

- The full cache mode runs the specified query and attempts to cache all the results. It executes this query very early to ensure that the first set of rows coming out of the source(s) are cached. If SSIS runs out of memory on the machine, the data flow fails, as the lookup component will not spool its memory overflow to disk. Once the data is cached, the lookup component will not go back to the database to retrieve its records, so long as the data flow is not restarted. In SQL Server 2008, lookup caches can be reused.

- The Lookup transformation is used to perform lookups by joining data in input columns with columns in a reference dataset. The reference dataset can be an existing table or view, a new table, a cache file, or the result of a SQL query. The lookup is used to access extra information in a related table that is based on values in common columns. Either an OLE DB connection manager or a Cache connection manager is used to connect to the referenced dataset. The Lookup transformation tries to perform an equi-join between values in the reference dataset and values in the transformation input. The lookups performed by the Lookup transformation are case sensitive.

- Data to be used in data warehouse must be extracted from the operational systems having the source data. The purpose of data extraction process is to bring all source data into a common, consistent format so that it is ready to be loaded into the warehouse.

- Validation errors may not be recognized until the data has been extracted from the operational systems. This can happen when data is extracted from multiple data sources. For example, reconciling data extracted from different sales tracking, shipping, and billing systems may discover inconsistencies that must be addressed in one or more source systems.

Pop Quiz

Q1: Which function is NOT provided by the SSIS designer?

Ans: Accessing metadata

Q2: What represents a dimension?

Ans: The time, 1st of December 2007 at 14:12:00

Plan the deployment of SSIS packages

- An Analysis Services Scripting Language (ASSL) script is an XML script of the metadata of an existing Analysis Services database which is generated by using SQL Server Management Studio. It is then run on another server to recreate the initial database. ASSL is used by client applications to communicate with Microsoft SQL Server Analysis Services (SSAS).

- Log providers are included in SQL Server Integration Services, which can be used to implement logging in packages, tasks, and containers. It is possible to capture run-time information with the help of logging. This helps a user to audit and troubleshoot a package every time it is executed. For example, with the help of a log, it is possible to capture the name of the operator who ran the package and the time the package began and finished. When a log is added to a package, the log provider and location of the log is chosen. The format for the log data is specified by the log provider.

- The package deployment utility is a folder that contains the files that are needed to deploy the packages in an Integration Services project on a different server. The deployment utility is created on the computer where the Integration Services project is stored. The content of the deployment folder is refreshed every time the project is built. This implies that any file saved to this folder that is not copied again to the folder by the build process will be deleted.

- The package deployment utility for an Integration Services project is created by first configuring the build process to create a deployment utility, and then building the project. When the project is built all the packages and package configurations in the project are automatically included. Additional files, such as Readme file, can be deployed with the project by placing the files in the Miscellaneous folder of the Integration

Services project. These files are automatically included when the project is built. Before building the project and creating the package deployment utility, the properties can be set on the deployment utility to customize the way the package in the project will be deployed.

Pop Quiz

Q1: What are the two modes of deployment for report server instances supported by SQL Server 2008 Reporting Services??

Ans: Native mode and Sharepoint integrated mode

Q2: Which is NOT optimized for SSIS 2008

Ans: .NET Connectivity

Design the configuration file for an SSIS package.

- An SQL Server 2005/2008 Integration Services (SSIS) package is made up of one or more tasks. If more than one task is present in the package, they are connected and sequenced by precedence constraints in the control flow. Tasks are control flow elements that define units of work that are performed in a package control flow.

- The custom tasks can also be written by using a programming language that supports a .NET programming language, such as C#, or COM, such as Visual Basic. The SSIS Designer provides the design surface for creating package control flow, and provides custom editors for configuring tasks.

- System variables and user-defined variables are the two types of variables supported by Integration Services. Useful information about package objects is provided by the system variables at runtime. Custom scenarios in packages are supported by user-defined variables. Both types of variables can be used in expressions, configurations, and scripts. The package-level variables include the pre-defined system variables available to a package and the user-defined variables with package scope.

- Variables are used to store values that a SQL Server Integration Services package and its containers, event handlers, and tasks can use at runtime. Variables can also be used by the scripts in the Script task and the Script component. The precedence constraints that sequence containers and tasks into a workflow can use variables when their constraint definitions include expressions.

Pop Quiz

Q1:   What are used to store values that a SQL Server Integration Services package and its containers, event handlers, and tasks can use at runtime?

Ans: Variables

Q2:   Which is made up of one or more tasks?

Ans: SQL Server 2005/2008 Integration Services (SSIS) package

Design a logging and auditing strategy.

- SSIS Designer is a graphical tool that is used to create and maintain SQL Server Integration Services (SSIS) packages. SSIS Designer is available in BIDS (Business Intelligence Development Studio) as part of an Integration Services project. SSIS Designer helps a user to perform the following tasks:

  - View the package content.

  - Construct the control flow in a package.

  - Construct the data flows in a package.

  - Add event handlers to the package and package objects.

  - View the execution progress of the package at runtime.

- The Sequence Container is one of the primary containers of SSIS 2008. It is used to organize the subsidiary tasks by grouping them together and lets a user apply transactions or allocate logging to the container.

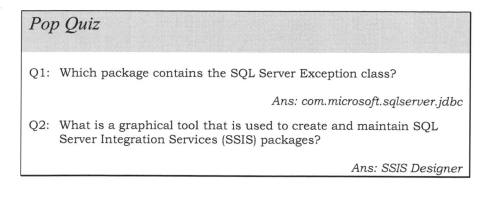

Pop Quiz

Q1: Which package contains the SQL Server Exception class?

Ans: com.microsoft.sqlserver.jdbc

Q2: What is a graphical tool that is used to create and maintain SQL Server Integration Services (SSIS) packages?

Ans: SSIS Designer

Test Your Knowledge

Q1. You work as a Database Administrator for uCertify Inc. The company uses a SQL Server 2008 database application and an OLE DB connection. You create a project named Customer. You notice that the connection string does not exist in the cache. What will you do?

    A.   Select & add a connection to the list of connection strings.

    B.   Create a new connection.

    C.   Create a new connection string.

    D.   Use the default connection string.

Q2. You work as a Database Developer for uCertify Inc. The company uses SQL Server 2008 as the database development platform. A project has been assigned to you to combine data from an Excel workbook and a table named Revenue in the SQL Server database. You have to then push the results to a fixed-width flat file.

What can you do to accomplish the task?

Each correct answer represents a complete solution. Choose all that apply.

    A.   Use the Import and Export Wizard.

    B.   Use Business Intelligence Development Studio (BIDS).

    C.   Combine data mining and data cleansing tasks.

    D.   Create a new package specifically for that purpose.

    E.   Modify the previously created package.

Q3. Which of the following tasks is used to execute a VB.NET or a C# .NET code in SSIS 2008?

    A.   Data Flow Task

    B.   Script Task

    C.   Execute SQL Task

    D.   Data Profiling Task

Q4. You work as a Database Administrator for uCertify Inc. You use a SQL Server 2008 database application to develop a Business Intelligence (BI) solution. You have to move a database from SQL Server 2000 to SQL Server 2008. You want to identify the data quality errors before carrying out data migration. You make use of the SQL Server Integration Services (SSIS) service to work out a solution which must meet the following requirements:

- Requires minimum development efforts.

- Runs as a repetitive process based on SSIS.

- Allows flexibility in patterns to identify NULL and invalid column values.

Which of the following SSIS tasks will you use to meet these requirements?

A.   Script task

B.   ActiveX Script task

C.   Data Profiling task

D.   Data Mining Query task

Q5. You manage a SQL Server 2008 server named uCert1. Users are complaining that the server has been responding very slowly and you suspect that a database application is encountering locking conditions. You want to check to see if any queries are being blocked. What should you check?

A.   SSRS

B.   SQL Server Error log

C.   Activity Monitor

D.   Windows application log

Answer Explanation

A1.   Answer option C is correct.

If a connection string does not exists in the cache, a new connection string is needed to be created. For example, to define a new connection string for an OLE DB connection take the following steps:

- Right click the Connection Managers pane and then click New OLE DB Connection.

- In the Configure OLE DB Connection Manager dialog box, click New.

- In the Provider list, choose from the list of OLE DB providers that are installed on the machine.

- Specify the database name and the connection security credentials, and then click OK.

- After specifying the connection options, one can choose the newly cached connection from the list which then adds the new connection to the Connection Managers pane in the package.

Answer option A is incorrect. Selecting & adding a connection to the list of connection strings does not add the connection string to the cache.

Answer option B is incorrect. Creating a new connection does not add the connection string to the cache.

Answer option D is incorrect. Using the default connection string does not add the connection string to the cache.

A2.   Answer options C, D, and E are correct.

This task needs combining the data merging and data cleansing tasks. Thus, you should either create a new package specifically for this purpose or modify a package created previously by the Import and Export Wizard.

Answer option A is incorrect. The Import and Export Wizard lets you work with a single source and a single destination.

Answer option B is incorrect. BIDS cannot be used to accomplish the task.

A3.   Answer option B is correct.

The Script Task within the SQL Server Integration Services (SSIS) service is used to execute a VB.NET or a C# .NET code. It has the following features:

- It uses the Visual Studio Tools for Applications 2.0 (VSTA) interface.

- It enables the user to run a VB.NET and a C# .NET code with the full host of methods and functions.

- It allows variables to be referenced and updated within a script.

- It allows connections to be referenced and updated within a script.

- It allows the SSIS breakpoints to be applied within the script's code (for the Script Task).

- It runs in both a 32-bit environment (X86) and a 64-bit environment (X64).

Answer option A is incorrect. The Data Flow Task allows data processing from sources to destinations. A package can have zero, one, or more data flows. To work with the Data Flow Task, a user can either drag a Data Flow Task from the Control Flow toolbox onto the workspace and then double-click it, or he can click the Data Flow tab within the SSIS Designer.

The Data Flow Task has three types of objects in the toolbox:

- Data flow source adapters

- Data flow transformations

- Data flow destination adapters

The following image shows the Data Flow tab with the toolbox:

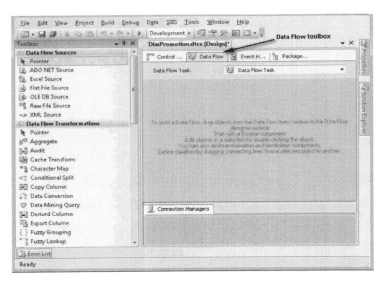

Answer option C is incorrect. The Execute SQL Task can run a stored procedure within SQL Server or any other relational database for which the user has an installed data provider. The syntax of the statements entered in the Execute SQL Task should be in a language native to the underlying database.

Answer option D is incorrect. The Data Profiling Task is used to review source data entities, to check the cleanliness and completeness of data, and to understand how the data is organized structurally, such as the possible key columns and the relationships between columns. It is used to gather the information about data including its accuracy, completeness, and statistics within the source tables or views.

The Data Profiling Task has two parts, which are as follows:

- The Data Profiling Task in the control flow that performs the analysis.

- The Data Profile Viewer that reviews the results. The Data Profile Viewer displays the results of the Data Profiling Task in a graphical form that demonstrates each profile type.

A4.   Answer option C is correct.

You will use the Data Profiling Task to meet the requirements. The Data Profiling Task is used to review source data entities, to check the cleanliness and completeness of data, and to understand how the data is organized structurally, such as the possible key columns and the relationships between columns. It is used to gather the information about data including its accuracy, completeness, and statistics within the source tables or views.

The Data Profiling Task has two parts, which are as follows:

- The Data Profiling Task in the control flow that performs the analysis.

- The Data Profile Viewer that reviews the results. The Data Profile Viewer displays the results of the Data Profiling Task in a graphical form that demonstrates each profile type.

Answer option A is incorrect. The Script Task within the SQL Server Integration Services (SSIS) service is used to execute a VB.NET or a C# .NET code. It has the following features:

- It uses the Visual Studio Tools for Applications 2.0 (VSTA) interface.

- It enables the user to run a VB.NET and a C# .NET code with the full host of methods and functions.

- It allows variables to be referenced and updated within a script.

- It allows connections to be referenced and updated within a script.

- It allows the SSIS breakpoints to be applied within the script's code (for the Script Task).

- It runs in both a 32-bit environment (X86) and a 64-bit environment (X64).

Answer option B is incorrect. The ActiveX Script task is used to run Microsoft Visual Basic Scripting Edition (VBScript) and JavaScript code. It is also included chiefly for legacy support when a Data Transformation Services (DTS) package is migrated to SQL Server Integration Services (SSIS).

Answer option D is incorrect. The Data Mining Query task performs data mining queries and allows a user to capture the results for analysis. The Data Mining Query task according to Analysis Services data mining models is built to run prediction queries. This task is similar to the Analysis Services Execute DDL task in which the user can execute subsequent mining queries against a processed mining model in Analysis Server.

A5.   Answer option C is correct.

Activity Monitor is a tool in SQL Server Management Studio (SSMS). It is used to get information about user connections to the database engine. It is also used to troubleshoot database locking issues and to terminate deadlocked or unresponsive processes. Blocking events can be observed in real-time in Activity Monitor. The Blocked By column in the Processes report will identify the source of the lock. A block occurs when an object is locked by one resource preventing other resources from accessing. An extreme example is when an application will create a lock on a resource just prior to requesting user input. Imagine a user needs to update a row in a table. If the application locks the row, then it waits for the user to input the information, and the row will remain locked until the user provides the input. If the user goes on break before inputting the data, the row will remain locked, and other users will be blocked from accessing the data. Unlike deadlocks, locks are not automatically detected and killed by SQL Server.

Answer option A is incorrect. SSRS stands for SQL Server Reporting Services. It creates and manages Web-enabled reporting services. It is used to create and generate reports, to retrieve data from various data sources, and to publish reports in various formats. SQL Server Reporting Services (SSRS) will serve reports, but it doesn't include error information on locking events.

Answer option B is incorrect. The SQL Server error log is used to ensure whether or not the processes regarding backup, restore, etc., have been completed. These processes include backup, restore, batch commands, and scripts. The SQL Server Error log can capture deadlock error events (including significant details if trace flags 1204 and/or 1222 are enabled), but it wouldn't capture locking events that aren't recognized as deadlocks.

Answer option D is incorrect. The Windows application log does not include information from locks.

Chapter 6 - Designing an Analysis Services Database

Overview

This chapter describes about the section of how to analyze cube performance, design cube architecture, design for international implementation, design a data source view, design and create business-driven, Multidimensional Expressions (MDX) calculations, and analyze cube performance.

Analyze cube performance

- Query Design tools are used to create queries in Report Designer of Reporting Services. The availability of a particular query designer depends on the kind of data that a user is working with. Moreover, some query designers provide alternate modes so that a user can choose whether to work in visual mode or directly in the query language. All of the query design tools run in the data design environment of BIDS (Business Intelligence Development Studio) when a user works with a Report Server Wizard project template or a Report Server project template. Some of the query design tools are as follows:

  - DMX Query Designer

  - MDX Query Designer

  - Generic Query Designer

  - Graphical Query Designer

  - Report Model Query Designer

- The Usage-Based Optimization Wizard is used to design aggregations for a partition. Aggregations are very efficient in reducing the query execution time and improving query response time by preparing the answers before the questions are asked.

- The Partitions cube designer tab is used to define the storage used for each measure group within a cube.

- In order to configure the default storage settings for new measure groups added to a cube, you should take the following two steps:

- On the Cube Builder tab in the Cube Wizard, click the cube object in either the Measures or Dimensions pane.

- In the Properties window, click the browse (...) button for the ProactiveCaching property setting..

Design cube architecture

- A cube is a set of dimensions and related measures, which is used to analyze data. It is synonymous with a Unified Dimensional Model (UDM).

- Dimension: It is a group of attributes that represent an area of interest related to the measures in the cube, and which are needed to analyze the measures in the cube.

- Measures: A measure is a fact, which is a measurement or transactional value that a user may want to aggregate.

- A cube is then augmented with calculations, key performance indicators (KPIs), actions, perspectives, partitions, and translations. A cube is created based on tables and views that are modeled in a data source view in Microsoft SQL Server 2005 Analysis Services (SSAS). It is possible to develop a cube with or without an underlying relational data source.

- Aggregations are pre-calculated summaries of data from leaf cells. They are very efficient in reducing the query execution time and improving query response time by preparing the answers before the questions are asked. Aggregations are used to provide performance improvements by allowing Microsoft SQL Server Analysis Services (SSAS) to retrieve pre-calculated totals directly from cube storage instead of recalculating data from an underlying data source for each query.

- The Cube Wizard is used to create a cube for a Microsoft SQL Server Analysis Services (SSAS) project in Business Intelligence Development Studio. To open this wizard in Business Intelligence Development Studio in Solution Explorer, right-click the Cubes folder for an Analysis Services project, and then click New Cube. After the Cube Wizard has been created, its properties can be modified by the Cube Designer in Business Intelligence Development Studio (BIDS).

- Dimensions, in Microsoft SQL Server Analysis Services (SSAS), are a fundamental component of cubes. Dimensions are used to organize data with relation to an area of interest, such as stores, customers, or employees, to users. In Analysis Services, dimensions contain attributes that correspond to columns in dimension tables. These attributes appear as attribute hierarchies. These attributes can be organized into user-defined hierarchies, or can be defined as parent-child hierarchies based on columns in the underlying dimension table.

- A Key Performance Indicator (KPI) in Microsoft SQL Server Analysis Services (SSAS) is a collection of calculations, which are associated with measure groups in a cube. These calculations are used to evaluate business success. Typically, these calculations are a combination of calculated members and Multidimensional Expressions (MDX) expressions.

- Additional metadata are also present in KPIs, which provide information about how client applications should display the result of a KPI's calculation. One prime advantage of the KPIs in Analysis Services is that they are server-based KPIs that are consumable by different client applications.

Pop Quiz

Q1: Which GROUP BY statement is NOT used to generate the execution plan?

Ans: GROUP BY...WITH PLAN

Q2: Which two models characteristics are combined by an SSAS cube?

Ans: Relational model and Dimensional model

Design for international implementation

- A named query in SSAS 2008 is a SQL expression represented as a table. The user can define a SQL expression in a named query to select rows and columns that are returned from one or more tables.

A named query is like any other table in a data source view with rows and relationships, except that it is based on an expression.

- A named query can be used to extend the relational schema of existing tables in a data source view without altering the primary data source. For example, named queries can be used in series to split up a complex dimension table into smaller, simpler dimension tables for use in database dimensions. The user can also use a named query to join multiple database tables from one or more data sources into a single data source view table.

- SSAS stands for SQL Server Analysis Services. It stores, processes, and secures data. It delivers OLAP (Online Analytical Processing) and data mining functionalities for business intelligence applications. It is used to design, create, and manage multi-dimensional structures that contain data aggregated from other data sources.

Pop Quiz

Q1: Which role is installed by the setup program when SQL Server Analysis Services (SSAS) is installed?

Ans: Administrators role

Q2: Which feature of SQL Server is used to monitor the performance of Microsoft SQL Server Analysis Services (SSAS)?

Ans: SQL Server Profiler

Design a data source view

- A data source in Microsoft SQL Server Analysis Services (SSAS) is used to represent a connection to a data source. A data source also contains a connection string that defines how Analysis Services connects to a physical data store by using a native OLE DB provider or a managed Microsoft .NET Framework.

- The connection string contains server name, database, timeout, security, and other connection-related information. Many data sources are directly supported by Analysis Services. Supported data sources comprise Microsoft SQL Server databases and databases created by other products, including DB2, Oracle, and Teradata. A user can define a new data source or define a data source based on a formerly defined data source.

- A data source view is a document that is used to describe the schema of an underlying data source. It provides destinations and lookup tables for SQL Server Integration Services tasks, transformations, data sources, and destinations. A data source view is built on a data source. A data source view, in Integration Services, is a design-time object that makes it simple to implement the same data source in multiple packages. It is also possible to extend a data source view. Data source views can be created in Business Intelligence Development Studio, Analysis Services, and in Integration Services projects.

- The relational data warehouse is a critical component of the Data Warehouse layer. It is ideally suited for the storage of data at the lowest level of granularity. The availability of such fine-grained data supports data maintenance, validation, and the flexible combination of data for specific forms of analysis.

Pop Quiz

Q1: Which statement is NOT true about monitoring SQL Server Analysis Services?

Ans: Performance is a Microsoft Management Control (MMC) snap-in that tracks data usage

Q2: Which action is used to let the clients request the details behind aggregated cell values in a cube?

Ans: Drillthrough actions

Design and create business-driven Multidimensional Expressions (MDX) calculations.

- The generic query designer is the default query building tool for most supported relational data sources, including Oracle, OLE DB, XML Web services, Microsoft SQL Server, and ODBC. In contrast with the graphical query designer, query syntax is not validated during query design by the generic query designer tool. This query designer is recommended for creating complex queries, stored procedures, for writing dynamic queries, and for querying XML data.

- The Report Model query designer is used to modify or create queries that run against a report model that has been published to a report server. Clickthrough data exploration is supported by the reports that run against models. The path of data exploration is determined by the query at run time. In order to use the Report Model query designer, data source that points to a published model should be defined. The Report Model query designer can be used in either graphical or generic mode.

- The MDX query designer is used for creating queries that run against an Analysis Services or other multidimensional data source. The MDX query designer becomes available when a dataset is created in Report Designer that uses SAP NetWeaver BI data source or Analysis Services.

- The DMX query designer is used to retrieve data from a data mining model. A user should have an Analysis Services data source that includes a data mining model if he wants to use the DMX query designer. After the model is selected, data mining prediction queries can be created that provides data to a report.

- The number of axes supported by the SELECT statement is up to 128 with each one of them formally named as Axis(n), where n is the number from 0 to 127. Within the SELECT statement, sets are assigned to axes using the ON keyword followed by the axes.

Pop Quiz

Q1: Which statement is included in the basic MDX query syntax?

Ans: SELECT

Q2: Which hierarchy has a different number of levels between the top and leaf levels?

Ans: Ragged hierarchy

Analyze cube performance

- MDX stands for Multidimensional Expressions. These expressions are units of code that can be evaluated to return a value or an object reference and are a critical part of various object properties and MDX statements.

- The MDX language is used to assemble tuples identifying points of data within an n-dimensional space. MDX lets the user query multidimensional objects, such as cubes, and return multidimensional cell sets that contain the data of the cube.

- Perspectives allow database administrators to provide various views of a cube. However, perspectives are not designed as a security structure because if the user knows how to write an MDX expression, he can always access any piece of a cube regardless of the currently effective perspective.

- When a perspective is defined, a user can choose the measure groups, measures, dimensions, attributes, hierarchies, calculations, and KPIs.

He then selects a specific perspective in order to restrict the elements available for analysis.

- Translations provide a multi-lingual aspect to cube data. SSAS is not a language translation engine. However, if the users provide this feature, SSAS allows them to select and browse cubes in their preferred language.

- Translations occur at two different levels - structure of a cube and source data. If the user wants to display the structural elements of a cube in a given language, he would embed the translation for the name of an object such as a dimension, hierarchy, or attribute in the definition of the cube. However, if he wants to display translations for members within a dimension, he would need to provide the translation within the source data and then map the translated columns to the appropriate attribute in the cube.

Pop Quiz

Q1:   Which statement is **NOT** true about the installation of SQL Server Analysis Services (SSAS)?

Ans: The SQL Server 2005 Analysis Services (SSAS) Instance Rename tool is supported for use in a cluster environment.

Q2:   Which action should you perform to install an additional instance of SSAS?

Ans: Run the Setup again and specify a unique name for the new instance.

Test Your Knowledge

Q1. You work as an Enterprise Application Developer for uCertify Inc. In the cube architecture, you have created new dimensions that are not automatically added to existing cubes. You have designed one or more new dimensions by using the Dimension Wizard rather than letting the Cube Wizard create them automatically.

You need to add your new dimensions to a cube to let the end users browse the cube data with the help of those dimensions. While using the Dimension Wizard, you inadvertently select the wrong primary key column and fail to select all the attributes you need for the dimension.

What will you do?

Each correct answer represents a part of the solution. Choose all that apply.

A. Delete the dimension.

B. Update the key attribute so that it re?ects the correct key columns property.

C. Specify the cubes to which the new dimension will be added after it is created.

D. Add the additional attributes as needed.

Q2. You work as an Administrator for TechSoft Inc. The company has a SQL Server 2005 computer that hosts a SSAS 2005 database. You have decided to install a named instance of SSAS 2008 on the same computer as SSAS 2005. You want to migrate the cubes from SSAS 2005 to SSAS 2008 in such a way that there is no effect on the SSAS 2005 installation. Which of the following approaches should you choose to accomplish the task?

A. In-place upgrade

B. Side-by-side migration

C. Out-place upgrade

D. Parallel migration

Q3. You work as a Database Administrator for uCertify Inc. The company uses SQL Server 2008 as the development platform for Business Intelligence (BI) solutions. You are assigned the task to analyze customers' interests for the various sections of the company's website. This information is stored in log files on the Web server which are then loaded onto the company's database. You plan to use a SQL Server 2008 Integration Services (SSIS) solution to enumerate these log files.

Which of the following control flow elements should you use to accomplish the task?

A.   The For Loop Container

B.   The Data Profiling Task

C.   The Foreach Loop Container

D.   The Sequence Container

Q4.   You work as a Database Administrator for uCertify Inc. The company uses the SQL Server 2008 database platform for creating a SQL Server 2008 Analysis Services (SSAS) solution. The SSAS solution uses a table named "Client". The table is stored in a source database named "dbsrc". You have read-only access to the source database. The "Client" table contains several columns. You need to reduce the number of columns in the "Client" table and split the table so that it can be distributed across multiple table definitions.

Which of the following actions will you perform to accomplish the task?

A.   Create multiple data sources for the SSAS solution.

B.   Create multiple database views for the source database "dbsrc".

C.   Create multiple data source views for the SSAS solution.

D.   Create multiple named queries for the SSAS solution.

Q5.   Which of the following Analysis Services objects contains a connection string that defines how Analysis Services connects to a physical data store by using a native OLE DB provider or a managed Microsoft .NET Framework?

A.   Data source

B.   Data source view

C.   Dimensions

D.   Mining structure

Answer Explanation

A1. Answer options A, B, and D are correct.

Although you can certainly delete the dimension and start over, it is likely that you can make all necessary corrections by using the Dimension Designer. Simply update the key attribute so that it re?ects the correct key columns property.

Answer option C is incorrect. You cannot specify the cubes to which a new dimension will be added.

A2. Answer option B is correct.

You should choose side-by-side migration to accomplish the task. As mentioned in the question, you have decided to install the named instance of SSAS 2008 on the same computer as SSAS 2005 without affecting the SSAS 2005 installation. Migration of SSAS cubes requires testing, adding a new client access provider, and making cube structure changes. Therefore, a place is needed to test and modify the new SSAS 2008 cubes. The side-by-side installation gives the user the flexibility to test the cubes after they have been migrated and processed.

Answer option A is incorrect. An in-place upgrade overwrites the existing SSAS 2000 installation with SSAS 2008 and can break client-tool access. Moreover, an in-place upgrade is used when a user installs SSAS 2008 on the same server as a default no-named instance of SSAS 2005. As the named instance of SSAS 2008 is installed, this is not the correct approach.

Answer options C and D are incorrect. There are no such approaches as out-place upgrade and parallel migration in SSAS.

A3. Answer option C is correct.

You should use the Foreach Loop Container to enumerate the log files that are stored on the Web server. The Foreach Loop Container is one of the primary containers of SSIS 2008. It allows looping, but instead of providing a condition expression, it loops over a set of objects such as files in a folder.

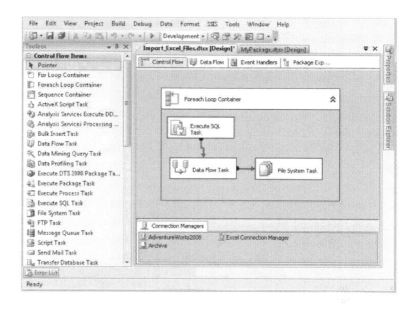

Note: Additionally, the user can drag task objects and other containers into his container.

Answer option A is incorrect. The For Loop Container cannot be used to accomplish the task. The For Loop Container is one of the primary containers of SSIS 2008. It provides the same functionality as the Sequence Container except that it also allows a user to run the tasks within it multiple times based on an evaluation condition, such as looping from 1 to 10.

Answer option B is incorrect. The Data Profiling Task cannot be used to accomplish the task. The Data Profiling Task is used to review source data entities, to check the cleanliness and completeness of data, and to understand how the data is organized structurally, such as the possible key columns and the relationships between columns. It is used to gather the information about data including its accuracy, completeness, and statistics within the source tables or views.

The Data Profiling Task has two parts, which are as follows:

- The Data Profiling Task in the control flow that performs the analysis.

- The Data Profile Viewer that reviews the results. The Data Profile Viewer displays the results of the Data Profiling

Task in a graphical form that demonstrates each profile type.

Answer option D is incorrect. The Sequence Container cannot be used to accomplish the task. The Sequence Container is one of the primary containers of SSIS 2008. It is used to organize the subsidiary tasks by grouping them together and lets a user apply transactions or allocate logging to the container.

A4. Answer option D is correct.

You should create multiple named queries for the SSAS solution. This helps to distribute the data across multiple table definitions. A named query in SSAS 2008 is a SQL expression represented as a table. The user can define a SQL expression in a named query to select rows and columns that are returned from one or more tables. A named query is like any other table in a data source view with rows and relationships, except that it is based on an expression.

A named query can be used to extend the relational schema of existing tables in a data source view without altering the primary data source. For example, named queries can be used in series to split up a complex dimension table into smaller, simpler dimension tables for use in database dimensions. The user can also use a named query to join multiple database tables from one or more data sources into a single data source view table.

Answer options A, B, and C are incorrect. These actions do not allow data distribution across multiple table definitions.

A5. Answer option A is correct.

A data source in Microsoft SQL Server Analysis Services (SSAS) is used to represent a connection to a data source. A data source also contains a connection string that defines how Analysis Services connects to a physical data store by using a native OLE DB provider or a managed Microsoft .NET Framework.

The connection string contains server name, database, timeout, security, and other connection-related information. Many data sources are directly supported by Analysis Services. Supported data sources comprise Microsoft SQL Server databases and databases created by other products, including DB2, Oracle, and Teradata. A user can define a new data source or define a data source based on a formerly defined data source.

Answer option B is incorrect. A data source view is a document that is used to describe the schema of an underlying data source. It provides destinations and lookup tables for SQL Server Integration Services tasks, transformations, data sources, and destinations. A data source view is built on a data source. A data source view, in Integration

Services, is a design-time object that makes it simple to implement the same data source in multiple packages. It is also possible to extend a data source view. Data source views can be created in Business Intelligence Development Studio, Analysis Services, and in Integration Services projects.

Answer option C is incorrect. Dimensions, in Microsoft SQL Server Analysis Services (SSAS), are a fundamental component of cubes. Dimensions are used to organize data with relation to an area of interest, such as stores, customers, or employees, to users. In Analysis Services, dimensions contain attributes that correspond to columns in dimension tables. These attributes appear as attribute hierarchies. These attributes can be organized into user-defined hierarchies, or can be defined as parent-child hierarchies based on columns in the underlying dimension table.

Answer option D is incorrect. The mining structure is a data structure that defines the data domain from which mining models are built. Multiple mining models that share the same domain can be present in a single mining structure. Columns are the building blocks of the mining structure. These columns describe the data contained in the data source and contain information such as content type, data type, and how the data is distributed. A mining structure can also contain nested tables, which represent a one-to-many relationship between the entity of a case and its related attributes. The information about how columns are used for a specific mining model, or about the type of algorithm used to build a model, is not present in the mining structure.

Section C
Full length Practice Test

Full Length Practice Test Questions

Test Your Knowledge

Q1. You work as a System Administrator for uCertify Inc. The company uses the Visual Studio user interface and executes queries on a SQL Server 2008 database. A project has been assigned to you to monitor the report server activity. You create a report in Business Intelligence (BI) Development Studio and the data is cached as an .rdl.data file, which is used when you preview the report.

To debug report problems, it is sometimes useful to prevent the refresh task for report data so that it does not change when you are debugging. You must ensure that only cached data is used by the BI Development Studio. What will you do to accomplish the task?

A.   Add a code with the cache value set to 0 to the configuration file in the BI Development Studio directory.

B.   Add a code with the cache value set to 1 to the configuration file in the BI Development Studio directory.

C.   Add a code with the cache value set to NULL to the configuration file in the BI Development Studio directory.

D.   Add a code with the cache value set to FALSE to the configuration file in the DI Development Studio directory.

Q2. You work as a System Administrator for uCertify Inc. The company uses the Visual Studio user interface and executes queries on a SQL Server 2008 database.

You are developing a report schema. The report schema will be deployed on the reporting server where users choose relevant fields and develop reports. Later, the users can download the reports locally.

Which type of report will you use to prepare the schema?

A.   Cached report

B.   Snapshot report

C.   Ad hoc report

D.   Linked report

Q3. You work as a database developer for uCertify Inc. The company uses Visual Studio .NET as its application development platform. You create a Windows-based application using .NET Framework 2.0. The application displays data from a SQL Server 2008 database. You are assigned the project of managing the data acquisition strategy. You prepare the following MDX query:

- WITH MEMBER Measures.x AS

- Customer.Education.Currentmember.Name

- SELECT Measures.x ON 0,

- Customer.City.Members ON 1

- FROM [Adventure Works]

Which of the following members is returned as a result of the query?

A.   A data member

B.   A leaf member

C.   A parent member

D.   An (All) member

Q4. You work as a Developer for TechMart Inc. The company has a SQL Server 2008 computer. You are creating a SQL Server 2008 Reporting Services (SSRS) Production report for the company. You have already defined the data sources and want to create a dataset for each data source. You also want to write a query using the query language of the data source. You do not want the query to be timed out. What should you do to accomplish the task?

Each correct answer represents a part of the solution. Choose all that apply.

A.   Select Text from the Command Type.

B.   Select Table from the Command Type.

C.   Leave the Timeout empty or type 0 sec.

D.   In Timeout, type 45 sec.

E.   In Timeout, type 50 sec.

F.   Select StoredProcedure from the Command Type.

Q5. You work as an Administrator for Softech Inc. The company has a SQL Server 2008 computer. You are managing a SQL Server 2008 Reporting Services (SSRS) solution. You realize that the Reporting Services data sources are burdened due to the creation and processing of many reports. For this reason, the report response time has also increased. You want to reduce the overhead of the Reporting Services data source and enhance its performance. Which of the following reports can help you to accomplish the task?

Each correct answer represents a complete solution. Choose all that apply.

A.   Report snapshot

B.   Cached report

C.   Parameterized report

D.   Drillthrough report

Q6. What are the core components of the SQL Server 2008 Reporting Services (SSRS)?

Each correct answer represents a complete solution. Choose all that apply.

A.   A tool set to create, view, and manage reports

B.   A Report Server component that hosts and processes reports

C.   An API

D.   A checkpoint

Q7. You work as a database developer for uCertify Inc. The company has a SQL Server 2008 computer. You are designing a SQL Server 2008 Reporting Services (SSRS) report. You notice that while printing the report, blank pages are printed after every page that contains the data. However, the report appears correctly when viewed on the screen. You want to ensure that the blank pages are not printed. Which of the following report properties should you use to accomplish the task?

A.   Page Size

B.   Grid Spacing

C.   Interactive Size

D.   Extent

Q8. You work as a Database Analyst for uCertify Inc. The company has a SQL Server 2008 database platform to develop various Business Intelligence (BI) solutions. You have created a SQL Server 2008 Reporting Services (SSRS) solution that contains a report named "SDetails". It keeps a record of the weekly sales of each employee.

The end users need to view the weekly sales details for each employee with the help of the "SSummary" report. You have to make sure that when the users click a value in the month column of the "SSummary" report, it opens the "SDetails" report. Which of the following resources will you use to accomplish the task?

A.   A subreport

B.   A bookmark link

C.   A drilldown report

D.   A drillthrough report link

Q9. Which of the following features of SQL Server 2008 are valid options for deploying a report?

Each correct answer represents a complete solution. Choose all that apply.

A.   BIDS

B.   The Computer Management Console

C.   The .NET START command

D.   SQL Server Management Studio

E.   Report Manager

Q10. You manage a SQL Server 2008 server within a domain named uCertify.com. You are deploying an instance of SQL Server Reporting Services (SSRS). SSRS needs to be usable as soon as possible. Plans are being developed to purchase and install Microsoft Office SharePoint Services (MOSS). When it is installed, SSRS will be integrated with MOSS. What mode should you use when installing SSRS?

A.   Deploy SSRS using SharePoint Integrated Mode.

B.   Deploy SSRS using Native Mode.

C.   Install the SSRS instance and select Install, But Do Not Configure the Report Server.

D.   Wait until MOSS is deployed before installing an instance of SSRS.

Q11. You work as a Database Developer for uCertify Inc. The company has a Windows Vista-based computer with Microsoft SQL Server 2008 installed on it. You open a database named Sales created in Microsoft SQL Server 2008. You are assigned the task to enhance the search operations. You want to retrieve information about the registered protocol handlers. Which of the following system stored procedures will you use to accomplish the task?

A.   SP_HELP_FULLTEXT_SYSTEM_COMPONENTS

B.   SP_FULLTEXT_SERVICE

C.   SP_FULLTEXT_TABLES_CURSOR

D.   SP_HELP_FULLTEXT_TABLES

Q12. Which of the following data mining processing objects reads and caches the training data in the structure?

A.   Process Structure

B.   Process Default

C.   Process Full

D.   Process Clear Structure

Q13. You work as an Administrator for Bluewell Inc. The company has a SQL Server 2008 computer. You manage a SQL Server 2008 Analysis Services database. Data mining is configured in the company, giving you access to the information you need to make intelligent decisions about difficult business problems.

The data mining has a mining structure named msSalesData. There are several mining models associated with it. You want to control only one of the mining models, named mm1SalesInfo, within your mining structure. What should you do?

Each correct answer represents a part of the solution. Choose all that apply.

A.   Process the msSalesData mining structure.

B.   Process the mm1SalesInfo mining model.

C.   Process the mining structure along with all its mining models.

D.   Process only the mm1SalesInfo mining model.

E.   Process only the msSalesData mining structure

Q14. You work as a Business Analyst for uCertify Inc. You and your team members develop a distributed application that processes orders from multiple clients. The application uses SQL Server 2008 to store data for all the orders. The application does not implement any custom performance counters. However, some validation errors are raised when the clients try to access their individual accounts. What will you do to identify these errors?

A.   Perform data extraction.

B.   Perform data integration.

C.   Perform data transformation.

D.   Perform data analysis.

Q15. You work as an Application Developer for uCertify Inc. A project has been assigned to you to design a multidimensional database. You design a data source view using the SQL Server 2008 Analysis Services (SSAS). You have to replace a table with another table. What will you do to accomplish the task?

Each correct answer represents a part of the solution. Choose all that apply.

A.   Have an active connection to the source data in Data Source View Designer in project mode.

B.   Replace the table and specify the renamed table as the source of the corresponding table in the data source view before refreshing the data source view.

C.   Delete the previous table and add a new table to the data source view.

D.   Alter the data source view using the ALTER_VIEW command.

Q16. Which of the following Data Flow Sources is used for staging data for mining?

A.   Excel Source

B.   OLE DB Source

C.   Raw File Source

D.   XML Source

Q17. Which of the following query designers is used to retrieve data from a data mining model?

A.   DMX

B.   MDX

C.   Generic query designer

D.   Graphical query designer

E.   Report Model query designer

Q18. Which of the following data mining algorithms can be used to arrange the products on shelves in a retail store?

A.   Association rules algorithm

B.   Naive Bayes algorithm

C.   Clustering algorithm

D.   Decision Trees algorithm

Q19. You work as an administrator for Bluewell Inc. The company has a SQL Server 2008 computer. You manage a Microsoft SQL Server 2008 Analysis Services (SSAS) instance. You deploy a data mining structure, which includes the Clustering mining model of Microsoft. You want to change the mining model properties from Scalable K-Means to Non-scalable K-Means. Which of the following parameters of the mining model should you change to accomplish the task?

A.   CLUSTERING_METHOD

B.   MODELLING_CARDINALITY

C.   CLUSTER_COUNT

D.   STOPPING_TOLERANCE

E.   SAMPLE_SIZE

Q20. Which of the following data mining algorithms is used to calculate the probabilities for each possible state of the input attribute, provided that each state of the predictable attribute is given?

A.   Naive Bayes

B.   Decision Trees

C.   Association Rules

D.   Clustering

Q21. You have just installed a default instance and a named instance of SQL Server 2008 on a server within your network. Users are unable to connect to any of the SQL Server 2008 instances. The command-line tool Ping shows that the clients have TCP/IP connectivity. What should you do?

A.   Open port 1434 on the server.

B.   Open ports 1433 and 1434 on the server.

C.   Configure the SQL Server Browser service.

D.   Configure the SQL Server Agent service.

Q22. You manage a SQL Server 2008 server named uCert1 that hosts the Exams database. You need to optimize queries executed on the server. What can you use to identify the queries that use the most CPU time?

A.   Use the sys.dm_exec_query_stats dynamic management view.

B.   Look for queries using query hints.

C.   Use SQL Server Agent to log the CPU time for all queries.

D.   Enable a SSRS trace.

Q23. You work as a Database Administrator for uCertify Inc. The company uses SQL Server 2008 as the platform to develop Business Intelligence (BI) solutions. You have created a SQL Server 2008 Analysis Services (SSAS) solution. This solution has two tables named "CustContact" and "CustDetails" which store the customer data. The BI solution utilizes the two data sources named "CustCont" that accesses the CustContact table and "Cust" that accesses the CustDetails table. These datasources belong to two different servers.

You intend to create a dimension named "DimCust" which analyzes the customer data. You have to make sure that the "DimCust" dimension represents the tables as a snowflake schema to include attributes from the two tables. What will you do to accomplish the task?

A.   Create a data source view that is associated with the "CustCont" and "Cust" datasources and add the tables to the data source view.

B.   Create a data source that is associated with the "CustCont" and "Cust" datasources and create a named query in the data source view.

C.   Create a data source that is associated with the "Cust" data source and add the "CustDetails" table to the datasource.

D.   Create a data source view that is associated with the "CustCont" data source and add the "CustContact" table to the datasource.

Q24. You work as a Database Administrator for uCertify Inc. You use SQL Server 2008 to develop a Business Intelligence (BI) solution. You create a SQL Server 2008 Reporting Services (SSRS) solution using Microsoft

Visual Studio .NET 2008. The SSRS solution contains a report named "ProductSale". You have to ensure that the report displays the following requirements:

- The total amount of year-wise sales for each product category

- The product category as rows and the corresponding year of sales as columns

- The number of years and the number of product categories for the report must be variable by nature.

Which of the following items should you add to accomplish the task?

A.   A subreport

B.   A tablix data region

C.   A matrix template

D.   A rectangle

Q25. You work as a Database administrator for uCertify Inc. The company uses the Itanium 64 bit operating system. You are given the task to monitor the execution of Integration Services packages that are running on Itanium servers and to manage the packages and folders in a hierarchical view. You upgrade an existing instance of SQL Server 2005 Integration Services to SQL Server 2008 Integration Services. However, you cannot transform the designs of the packages to load them into the Integration Services. What is the most likely cause of this problem?

A.   The Client Tools Backward Compatibility feature is not installed.

B.   The configuration file is not modified.

C.   The registry key that specifies the package location is not. modified.

D.   The package designing feature is not supported on the Itanium 64-bit operating system.

Q26. **You work as an administrator for Bluewell Inc. The company has a SQL Server 2008 computer. You are managing a SQL Server 2008 Integration Services (SSAS) package. You want to migrate DTS packages to SSIS with the help of the Package Migration Wizard. Which of the following can you use to start the Package Migration Wizard?**

Each correct answer represents a complete solution. Choose all that apply.

A. BIDS

B. SSMS

C. OLAP

D. DSV

Q27. You work as a database administrator for uCertify Inc. The company has a Windows Vista-based computer with SQL Server 2008 installed on it. The computer contains a database named Human Resource created in Microsoft SQL Server 2008. The database backup is taken every hour. There are frequent changes made in the database information. What should be the configuration of the full recovery model settings?

Each correct answer represents a part of the solution. Choose all that apply.

A. Under the full recovery model, schedule differential backups before and after full database backups.

B. Under the full recovery model, schedule differential backups between full backups.

C. Under the full recovery model, schedule partial backups.

D. Under the full recovery model, schedule frequent log backups.

Q28. You work as a Database Administrator for uCertify Inc. You use SQL Server 2008 Analysis Service (SSAS) services to develop a data mining solution which collects data from two separate operational source systems. It is noticed that when these operational systems are accessed directly, performance problems occur. The solution is updated daily by using current data. You have to integrate data for the data mining solution without causing performance problems.

Which of the following steps will you take to accomplish the task?

A. Collect the data directly from the operational sources and integrate it into a data source view.

B. Use SQL Server Integration Services (SSIS) to build a staging area to collect data from operational systems.

C. Create views in SQL Server 2008 to join the tables of all operational systems using OPENROWSET Query functions.

D.   Create views in SQL Server 2008 to join the tables of all
        operational systems using Linked Servers.

Q29. Which of the following data types in SQL Server 2008 is used to store
planar spatial data and perform operations on it?

A.   Geography data type

B.   Geometry data type

C.   Hierarchyid data type

D.   Filestream data type

Q30. Which of the following data types in SQL Server 2008 can be used to
store **unstructured** data, such as videos, graphic files, Word
documents, and Excel spreadsheets?

A.   Date and time data type

B.   Hierarchyid data type

C.   Spatial data type

D.   Filestream data type

Q31. You work as an administrator for Softech Inc. The company has a SQL
Server 2008 computer. You are designing a Microsoft SQL Server 2008
Integration Services (SSIS) package. You have created a table and
inserted the required data into the table. You receive an error message
"destination table not found" when you run the package without the
package destination objects.

You want to set the package property that executes the package
without giving the "destination table not found" error message when
the configuration setting of the Connection Manager fails. Which of the
following package properties should you set to accomplish the task?

A.   Set the DelayValidation property to true.

B.   Set the FailPackageOnFailure property to false.

C.   Set the SuspendRequired property to true.

D.   Set the NoDestination property to false.

Q32. You are hired as a Database Administrator by uCertify Inc. The company uses Visual Studio .NET as its application development platform. You create a Windows application using .NET Framework 2.0. The application contains a method that executes a stored procedure which has the employee information in an MS-SQL Server 2008 database.

You configure Lookup Transformations in a 32-bit environment to cache the reference data before the information in the input column is processed. The data is retrieved from flat files. The caching mode used is Partial mode. What will happen to the query?

A.   The lookup executes one query for each row in the pipeline against the reference data source.

B.   The lookup searches the cache for a match. If a match is not found, the pipeline row is redirected as configured.

C.   The disk read operation is performed once, and the query is cached in memory.

D.   During the pre-execution phase, the query is loaded from the data source and held in memory for the lookup process.

Q33. You work as an Administrator for TechMart Inc. The company has a SQL Server 2008 computer. You manage a SQL Server 2008 Analysis Services (SSAS) database for the company. You want to set the storage mode in such a way that the setting is normally used for a data source when there is a requirement of daily updates. Which of the following standard storage settings should you choose to accomplish the task?

A.   Scheduled MOLAP

B.   Medium Latency MOLAP

C.   Automatic MOLAP

D.   Low Latency MOLAP

Q34. Which of the following processing options for OLAP (Online Analytical Processing) objects is used to delete the partition data and apply Process Default to the cube dimension?

A.   Process Structure

B.   Process Data

C.   Process Full

D.   Process Default

Q35. You work as a Database Administrator for uCertify Inc. The company uses the SQL Server 2008 platform to develop a Business Intelligence (BI) solution. You create a cube that has a measure named Sales, which stores the customer sales data of the last six months.

This cube has a single partition having the storage property set to real-time hybrid online analytical processing (HOLAP). Queries against the cube must return the sales data entered an hour before the cube processing. The partition takes more than two hours to process the queries. What should you do to improve the cube processing and query response time?

    A.   Create a partition for each month and set the storage setting of the partition for the current month to low-latency multidimensional online analytical processing.

    B.   Modify the storage setting of the partition to multidimensional online analytical processing (MOLAP).

    C.   Create a partition for each customer and set the storage setting of every partition to low-latency multidimensional online analytical processing.

    D.   Modify the storage setting of the partition to real-time relational online analytical processing (ROLAP).

Q36. You work as an Administrator for Softech Inc. The company has a SQL Server 2008 computer named SQL1. You are managing a SQL Server 2008 Reporting Services solution for the company. You have installed a second instance of the Reporting Services and named it as Inst1. Which of the following syntaxes correctly represents the default Report Manager URL for a named instance of Reporting Services?

    A.   http://[SQL1]/Reports_[Inst1]

    B.   http://[SQL1]/Reports

    C.   http:// Reports/Reports_[Inst1]/ [SQL1]

    D.   http://Reports_[Inst1]/ [SQL1]

Q37. What are the different types of control flow elements provided by the SQL Server 2008 Integration Services (SSIS)?

Each correct answer represents a complete solution. Choose all that apply.

    A.   Containers

    B.   Tasks

C.   Precedence constraints

D.   Transformations

Q38. You work as an Administrator for Bluewell Inc. The company has a SQL Server 2008 computer. You are designing a Microsoft SQL Server 2008 Integration Services (SSIS) package. The package has three Data Flow tasks and three Control Flow tasks. You want the package to use a single transaction for all the tasks. You also need to configure the package and enlist these tasks into the same transaction. What should you do?

Each correct answer represents a part of the solution. Choose all that apply.

A.   Change the TransactionOption property to Supported for the package.

B.   Change the TransactionOption property to Required for the package.

C.   Change the TransactionOption property to Supported for each Data Flow task.

D.   Change the TransactionOption property to Required for each Data Flow task.

E.   Change the TransactionOption property to Supported for each Control Flow task.

F.   Change the TransactionOption property to Required for each Control Flow task.

Q39. You work as a Developer for Techmart Inc. The company has a SQL Server 2008 computer. You are designing a Microsoft SQL Server 2008 Integration Services (SSIS) package. There are 40 Data Flow tasks and 40 Control Flow tasks in the package. The package execution speed is slower than expected. You want to capture the start, finish, and elapsed time for the validation and execution of the package. What should you do to accomplish the task?

A.   Monitor the Progress tab during the execution of the package, and then monitor the Execution Results tab.

B.   Enable the OnProgress event handler.

C.   It is not possible to capture the start, finish, and elapsed time for the validation and execution of the package.

D.   Enable the checkpoint in the package.

Q40. You work as an Administrator for TechMart Inc. The company has a SQL Server 2008 computer. You manage a SQL Server 2008

Integration Services (SSIS) package. You want to enable the package transaction and want a series of tasks to be completed as a single unit. In this unit, either all the tasks should be successful and committed or an error is generated and none of the tasks are committed. What should you do to accomplish the task?

Each correct answer represents a part of the solution. Choose all that apply.

A.   Start the MSDTC service.

B.   Place the task within the Sequence Container.

C.   Set the TransactionOption property of the container to Required.

D.   Set the TransactionOption property of the container to Supported.

E.   Set the TransactionOption property of the container to NotSupported.

Q41.   You work as a Business Information Analyst for uCertify Inc. You create a project using Business Intelligence Service, which first creates a csv file from the database with a dynamic name containing the current date. You create a dynamic file named MyFile with a package scope "c:\". You are using an expression for the localpath where the complete filename is created. However, when you use this expression, the "failed to lock variable" error is raised.

Which of the following is the most likely cause of this problem?

A.   The Fullpath is specified via expressions, not via variables.

B.   The FTP service supports only static variables.

C.   There is a conflict when different threads try to access the same variable.

D.   The package scope is incorrect.

Q42. Which of the following are the primary containers in SQL Server Integration Services (SSIS) 2008?

Each correct answer represents a part of the solution. Choose all that apply.

A.   Foreach Loop container

B.   Sequence container

C.   Series container

D.   For Loop container

E.   Looping container

Q43. You work as an administrator for Techsoft Inc. The company has a SQL Server 2008 computer. You manage a Microsoft SQL Server 2008 Analysis Services (SSAS) instance, which has a cube. One day, employees of the company complain that the queries run slowly. You need to identity these queries and change the storage configuration of the cube. What should you do to accomplish the task?

A.   Run the Usage-Based Optimization Wizard to analyze and design aggregations.

B.   Run the Cube Wizard to analyze and design aggregations.

C.   Use SQL Profiler to examine the execution plans to analyze and design aggregations.

D.   It is not possible to identify slow running queries by analyzing aggregations.

Q44. Which of the following tabs of the cube designer is used to define the storage used for each measure group within a cube?

A.   Partitions

B.   Perspectives

C.   KPIs

D.   Actions

Q45. You work as an Administrator for Bluewell Inc. The company has a SQL Server 2008 computer and SQL Server 2008 Analysis Services (SSAS). The server has a table named Employees. A cube is created to analyze the data and enhance the data retrieval from the Employees table. New measure groups are added to the cube. You want to configure the default storage settings for the new measure groups added to a cube. What should you do?

Each correct answer represents a part of the solution. Choose all that apply.

A.   On the Cube Builder tab in the Cube Wizard, click the cube object in either the Measures or Dimensions pane.

B.   In the Properties window, click the browse (...) button for the ProactiveCaching property setting.

C.   On the Partitions tab in the Cube Wizard, expand the measure group and click the Storage Settings link for that measure group.

D.   Right-click the partition, and then click Storage Settings.

Q46. You work as an Administrator for Softech Inc. The company has a SQL Server 2008 computer. You manage a SQL Server 2008 Analysis Services (SSAS) database. Multiple queries are captured by the SSAS server for analysis. You want to trace how frequently queries are captured by the SSAS server. Which of the following SSAS Server Logging properties should you use to accomplish the task?

A.   Log\Query\CreateQuery-LogTable

B.   Log\QueryLog\QueryLogSampling

C.   Log\QueryLog\QueryLog-ConnectionString

D.   Log\QueryLog\ QueryLog-TableName

Q47. You work as an Administrator for TechSoft Inc. The company has a SQL Server 2008 computer. You are managing SQL Server 2008 Analysis Services (SSAS). There are many objects in SSAS and you want to control the execution of the processing job. Which of the following processing settings should you choose to accomplish the task?

A.   Parallel

B.   Sequential

C.   Writeback Table Option

D.   Default

Q48. You work as an Administrator for TechMart Inc. The company has a SQL Server 2008 computer. You are managing SQL Server 2008 Analysis Services (SSAS) for the company. The Analysis Services uses the Dimension Key Errors Processing Settings to determine the action taken by the Analysis Services when an error occurs during processing. Which of the following options should you set when a key value exists in a partition but does not exist in the corresponding dimension?

A.   Key not found

B.   Duplicate key

C.   Null key converted to unknown

D.   Null key not allowed

Q49. You work as an administrator for Softech Inc. The company has a SQL Server 2008 computer that has a database named Employees. You manage the SQL Server Analysis Services for the company. The dimension in a cube is configured to analyze the data of the Employees database. You need to store the data in the dimension. Which of the following storage modes are supported by the dimension?

Each correct answer represents a complete solution. Choose all that apply.

A.   MOLAP

B.   ROLAP

C.   HOLAP

D.   OLAP

Q50. You work as an Administrator for Bluewell Inc. The company has a SQL Server 2008 computer. You are managing a SQL Server 2008 Analysis Services (SSAS). You want to add new cubes and dimensions to an SSAS solution. Which of the following SQL Server tools should you use to accomplish the task?

Each correct answer represents a complete solution. Choose all that apply.

A.   BIDS Cube Wizard

B.   BIDS Dimension Wizard

C.   BIDS Cube Designer

D.   BIDS Dimension Designer

Answer Explanation

A1.   Answer option B is correct.

When a report is created in Business Intelligence Development Studio, the authoring client caches data as a .rdl.data file, which is used when the report is previewed. Every time the query changes, the cache is updated. To debug report problems, it is sometimes needed to prevent the refresh task for report data so that it does not change while debugging.

To ensure that BI Development Studio can use only cached data, add the following code to the devenv.exe.config file in the BI Development Studio directory.

<system.diagnostics>

<switches>

<add name="Microsoft.ReportDesigner.ReportPreviewStore.ForceCache" value="1" />

</switches>

</system.diagnostics>

As long as the value is set to 1, only cached report data is used. This section should be removed after the report debugging.

A2.   Answer option C is correct.

You will use the ad hoc report to prepare the schema. An ad hoc report is a report that can be created using an existing report model with the help of Report Builder. These reports refer chiefly to reports of Report Builder and not to reports that can be created with the use of the Report Wizard. Ad hoc reports control report models and pre-defined templates to enable information workers to quickly and easily explore business data using familiar terminology and data structures implemented in the report model. These reports can be saved and run locally or published to a report server, just like other reports in the Reporting Services.

Note: SQL Server 2008 reporting services support Ad-hoc reports.

Answer option A is incorrect. A cached report is a saved copy of a processed report. Cached reports improve performance by reducing the number of processing requests to the report processor. They also reduce the time required to retrieve reports of large sizes.

Answer option B is incorrect. A snapshot contains information related to layout and query results that were retrieved at a certain time. On-demand reports get up-to-date query results, whereas report snapshots are processed and then saved to a report server on the basis of a schedule. When a snapshot report is selected for viewing, the report server retrieves the stored report from the database and shows the data and layout that were current for the report at the time the snapshot was created.

Answer option D is incorrect. A linked report is an item of the Report Server that supplies an access point to an existing report. Typically, it is analogous to a shortcut that can be used to open a file. A linked report is the derivative of an existing report. It always inherits layout and data source properties from the original report. All other properties may not be the same as that original report including security, parameters, subscriptions, and schedules.

A3.   Answer option D is correct.

The (All) member is the calculated value of all members in an attribute hierarchy or a user-defined hierarchy. In the above query, an (All) member ("All Customers") is returned, because there is no relationship between Education and City. Therefore, the (All) member of the Education attribute hierarchy would be the default member of the hierarchy used in any tuple having the City attribute hierarchy where an Education member is not provided explicitly.

Answer option A is incorrect. A data member is a child member that is related to a parent member in a parent-child hierarchy. A data member, instead of holding the aggregate value for the parent's children, holds the data value for its parent member.

Answer option B is incorrect. A leaf member is a member of a hierarchy with no children.

Answer option C is incorrect. A parent member holds the aggregate value of its children.

A4.   Answer options A and C are correct.

A dataset is used to specify fields from the data source that a user plans to use in a report, as well as calculated fields that he can create. Datasets are created for each data source after data sources are being defined in the reports of the Reporting Services. A dataset also contains a pointer to the data source, parameters, and data options that include character sensitivities including case, width, kana type, accent, and collation information. The way, a user specifies data that he wants, depends on the data source itself. All datasets created for a report definition appears in the Report Dataset window. A report can have one or more datasets.

Following steps should be taken to create a dataset:

- In Data view, from Dataset, select New Dataset. This will open a new Dataset dialog box.

- Type a name in Name for the dataset on the Query tab.

- Select a data source from Data Source.

- Select the form that the query will take from the Command Type as follows:

- Select Text to write a query using the query language of the data source.

- Select Table to return all the fields in a relational database table.

- Select StoredProcedure to execute a stored procedure by name.

In Query String, type the query, table name, or stored procedure. It is possible to leave the Query String blank and build a query in Data view.

Type the number of seconds in Timeout, which represents the number of seconds the report server waits for a response from the database. The default value is 30 seconds in SQL Server 2005. The value in the Timeout must be greater than 0 or should be left empty. If it is left empty, the query will not time out.

Note: The default value of Timeout is 0 second in SQL Server 2008.

Then click OK.

A5.   Answer options A and B are correct.

Snapshot and cached reports can help to reduce the processing pressure on data sources and improve report response time. A report snapshot is a report that contains layout information and query results that were retrieved at a specific point in time. Report snapshots are processed on a schedule and then saved to a report server. When a user selects a report snapshot for viewing, the report server retrieves the stored report from the report server database. The report server also shows the data and layout that were current for the report at the time the snapshot was created.

Report snapshots are not saved in a particular rendering format. Instead, report snapshots are rendered in a final viewing format (such as HTML) only when an application or a user requests it. Deferred rendering makes a snapshot portable. The report can be rendered in the correct format for the Web browser or the requesting device.

A saved copy of a processed report is a cached report. Performance is improved with the help of cached reports by reducing the time required to retrieve large reports and by reducing the number of processing requests to the report processor. Cached reports have a mandatory expiration period, usually in minutes.

Answer option C is incorrect. A parameterized report uses input values to complete data or report processing. With the help of a parameterized report, a user can vary the output of a report based on values that are set when the report executes. Parameterized reports are frequently used for linked reports, drillthrough reports, and subreports, and connecting and filtering reports with related data.

Answer option D is incorrect. Drillthrough reports are the standard reports that are accessed through a hyperlink on a text box in the original report. Drillthrough reports work with a main report and are the target of a drillthrough action for a report item such as a chart or a placeholder text. The summary information is displayed by the main report, for example in a chart or matrix. Actions that are defined in the chart or matrix provide drillthrough links to reports that display greater details based on the aggregate in the main report. It is possible to filter a drillthrough report with the help of parameters.

A6.   Answer options A, B, and C are correct.

The core components of the SQL Server Reporting Services are as follows:

- A complete tool set that can be used to create, view, and manage reports.

- An API that allows developers to extend and integrate report and data processing in custom applications, or create custom tools to manage and build reports.

- A Report Server component that is able to host and process reports in a variety of formats. Output formats include HTML, TIFF, Excel, CSV, PDF, and more.

Answer option D is incorrect. Checkpoints are used in SQL Server Integration Services (SSIS) and not in SSRS. Checkpoints work together with transactions to enable package restartability. The unit of work that needs to be completed successfully in order for the data to be applied is called transaction. In the SQL Server Integration Services (SSIS) instead of running the whole package, failed packages can be started from the point of failure called checkpoints. Information about the packages execution is written to the checkpoint file only if a package is configured to use the checkpoints. This checkpoint file is used to restart the package from the point of failure when the failed package is rerun. The checkpoint file gets deleted if the package runs successfully, and then recreated the next time when the package runs.

A7.   Answer option A is correct.

In order to accomplish the task, you should use the Page Size property of the SQL Server Reporting Services. Page Size properties are used by the PDF and Image rendering extensions to establish the regular occurrence of page breaks based on a physical measurement. So you can set the page breaks with the help of the Page Size to prevent the printing of the blank pages.

Answer option B is incorrect. Grid spacing specifies the spacing between the grid lines. The up and down arrows are used to adjust the grid spacing. A grid is a two-dimensional structure made up of a series of intersecting vertical and horizontal axes used to structure content. It serves as a framework on which a designer can organize text and images in a rational, easy to absorb manner.

Answer option C is incorrect. Interactive Size is used by the HTML rendering extension to provide the equivalent of Page Size. The report server uses different properties to support pagination on dynamic pages because the HTML rendering extension dynamically resizes a report to accommodate drillthrough, drilldown, and show/hide features.

Answer option D is incorrect. An extent is the basic unit of allocation for tables and indexes. It is a block of eight contiguous pages, each page of 8 KB, thus totaling 64 KB in size. SQL Server has two types of extents:

- Uniform extent: In uniform extent, all eight pages in the extent are used by the same object.

- Mixed extent: In mixed extent, each of the eight pages in the extent can be used by a different object that are too small to take up all the pages present in one extent.

A8.   Answer option D is correct.

You should use a drillthrough report link to make sure that when the users click a value in the month column of the "SSummary" report, it opens the "SDetails" report. Drillthrough reports are standard reports that are accessed through hyperlinks on a text box in the original report. These reports work with a main report and are the target of a drillthrough action for a report item such as placeholder text or a chart. The main report displays summary information, for example, in a chart. Actions defined in the chart provide drillthrough links to reports that display greater details based on the aggregate in the main report. Drillthrough reports are not displayed within the original report.

Answer option A is incorrect. A subreport cannot be used for this purpose. A subreport is similar to a frame in a Web page. A subreport is a report that displays another report inside the body of a main report. In other words, it is used to embed another report within a report. Any report can be used as a subreport. The subreport can use different data sources than the main report. Subreports are typically used within a main report as a briefing book or as a container for a collection of related reports.

Answer option B is incorrect. A bookmark link cannot be used for this purpose.

Answer option C is incorrect. A drillthrough report cannot be used for this purpose. Drilldown reports enable the user to toggle conditionally report items that are hidden to control how much detail data they want to see. Drilldown reports initially hide complexity. These reports retrieve all possible data that can be shown in the report.

A9.   Answer options A and E are correct.

Business Intelligence Development Studio (BIDS) is Microsoft Visual Studio 2008 with additional project types that are specific to SQL Server business intelligence. BIDS is the main environment that a user will use to develop business solutions that include Integration Services, Analysis Services, and Reporting Services projects. Business Intelligence Development Studio is basically a development tool that is used to create reports, packages, and analysis projects. This tool contains projects and wizards to create the reports, packages and analysis projects either automatically or manually.

Report Manager is a Web-based report access and management tool that can be used to administer a single report server instance from a remote location over an HTTP connection. Report Manager can also be used for its report viewer and navigation features.

Answer option B is incorrect. The Computer Management Console cannot be used to deploy a report.

Answer option C is incorrect. The .NET START command cannot be used to deploy a report.

Answer option D is incorrect. SSMS cannot be used to deploy a report. SQL Server Management Studio (SSMS) is a combination of various graphical tools such as Query Analyzer, Enterprise Manager, and Analysis Manager. SSMS is used to access, configure, manage, administer, and develop all the objects and components of SQL Server.

A10.   Answer option B is correct.

When installing SQL Server Reporting Services, a user has three choices for the reporting Services Configuration:

- Native Mode: Setup will install the report server and configure it in the Native mode using default values, and the report server will be usable as soon as setup is finished.

- Integrated Mode: Setup will create the report server database in the SharePoint integrated mode, but the report server will not be available until a SharePoint product is installed and configured.

Install, but do not configure the report server: Setup will install SSRS, but the Reporting Services Configuration tool must be used to configure SSRS after the installation is finished.

Since the report server will be usable as soon as Setup is finished, if you choose the Native Mode during the installation, Native Mode is the best choice for the scenario.

Answer option A is incorrect. SharePoint integrated mode enables the integration of Reporting Services with the SharePoint databases and security model. These features become available when a user configures a report server to run within a larger deployment of a SharePoint 3.0 product or technology. This mode requires additional software and configuration. It also necessitates that a report server instance be dedicated for integrated operations. The benefit of doing this is a rich level of integration that allows a user to access and manage report server content types using the application pages and data stores of a SharePoint Web application. Since Microsoft Office SharePoint Services (MOSS) is not currently installed, SSRS would not be usable if SharePoint Integrated Mode is selected. It is possible to switch modes after MOSS is installed - the only limitation is that it is not possible to migrate data between the two modes.

Answer option C is incorrect. If you choose Install, But Do Not Configure the Report Server during the installation, it will take additional configuration before SSRS is ready.

Answer option D is incorrect. It is not necessary to wait until MOSS is deployed to take advantage of SSRS. SSRS can be installed and used almost immediately.

A11.   Answer option A is correct.

You will use the SP_HELP_FULLTEXT_SYSTEM_COMPONENTS procedure to accomplish the task. The sp_help_fulltext_system_components stored procedure is used to retrieve information about the registered word-breakers, filters, and protocol handlers.

Syntax:

sp_help_fulltext_system_components

{ 'all' | [@component_type =] 'component_type' }

, [@param =] 'param'

arguments:

all': This argument returns the information for all full-text components.

[@component_type =] component_type: This argument specifies the type of component.

[@param =] param: Based on component type, this can be one of the following: a locale identifier (LCID), the file extension with "." prefix, the full component name of the protocol handler, or the full path to the component DLL.

Answer option B is incorrect. The SP_FULLTEXT_SERVICE procedure is used to retrieve information related to the properties of the Full-Text Engine and to change the properties for the MS Full-Text Search service.

Syntax:

sp_fulltext_service [[@action=] 'action'

[, [@value=] value]]

Arguments:

[@action=] 'action': It is the property to be changed or reset.

[@value=] value: It is the value of the specified property.

Answer option C is incorrect. The SP_FULLTEXT_TABLES_CURSOR stored procedure is used to return a list of those tables that are registered for full-text indexing by using a cursor.

Answer option D is incorrect. The SP_HELP_FULLTEXT_TABLES stored procedure returns a list of tables that are registered for full-text indexing.

Syntax:

sp_help_fulltext_tables   [[@fulltext_catalog_name   =   ] 'fulltext_catalog_name']

[, [@table_name =] 'table_name']

Arguments:

[@fulltext_catalog_name =] 'fulltext_catalog_name': It is the full-text catalog name. fulltext_catalog name is sysname, with a default value NULL.

If fulltext_catalog_name is omitted or is NULL, all full-text indexed tables that are associated with the database are returned. If fulltext_catalog_name is specified, but table_name is omitted or is NULL, the full-text index information is retrieved for every full-text indexed table that is associated with this catalog. If both fulltext_catalog_name and table_name are specified, a row is returned if table_name is associated with fulltext_catalog_name; otherwise, an error is raised.

[@table_name =] 'table_name': It is the name of the one- or two-part table for which the full-text metadata is requested.

A12.   Answer option A is correct.

The Process Structure processing objects reads and caches the training data in the structure.

The different data mining processing options are described in the following table:

Processing Options	Description
Unprocess	It deletes data from the mining object.

Process Default	It performs the minimum number of tasks that are required to fully initialize a mining object.
Process Structure	It reads and caches the training data in the structure. It does not affect the mining models inside the structure.
Process Full	It drops the object stores and rebuilds the model. This option is required by metadata changes, such as adding a new column to a mining structure.
Process Clear Structure	It drops the cached data without affecting the mining models inside the structure. It also disables the drillthrough features.

A13.   Answer options A and B are correct.

As mentioned in the question, you want to process only one of the mining models, named mm1SalesInfo, within the msSalesData mining structure. You should take the following two steps to accomplish this task:

- Firstly, process the msSalesData mining structure.

- Then process the mm1SalesInfo mining model.

- To control how the models are processed within your mining structure, you can process a mining structure separately from its associated mining models.

Answer option C is incorrect. As mentioned in the question, you want to process only one mining model named mm1SalesInfo; therefore, you should not process all the mining models, as it will enhance the administrative effort.

Answer option D is incorrect. You should also process the mining structure msSalesData before processing the mm1SalesInfo mining model.

Answer option E is incorrect. Processing the mining structure without processing the mining model will not serve the purpose.

A14.   Answer option A is correct.

Data to be used in data warehouse must be extracted from the operational systems having the source data. The purpose of data extraction process is to bring all source data into a common, consistent format so that it is ready to be loaded into the warehouse.

Validation errors may not be recognized until the data has been extracted from the operational systems. This can happen when data is extracted from multiple data sources. For example, reconciling data extracted from different sales tracking, shipping, and billing systems may discover inconsistencies that must be addressed in one or more source systems.

Answer option B is incorrect. Microsoft SQL Server 2008 provides a scalable enterprise data integration platform with excellent Extract, Transform, Load (ETL), and integration capabilities. These capabilities facilitate organizations to handle data from a wide range of data sources. This data is converted into an Integration Services data type when it enters a data flow in a package. If data has a data type that is not convertible to an Integration Services data type, an error occurs.

Numeric data is allocated a numeric data type, string data is allocated a character data type, and dates are allocated a date data type. Other data, such as GUIDs and Binary Large Object Blocks (BLOBs), are also allocated suitable Integration Services data types.

Answer option C is incorrect. Validation errors cannot be identified by data transformation.

Answer option D is incorrect. Validation errors cannot be identified by data analysis.

A15.   Answer options A and B are correct.

A table in a data source view can be replaced with a different table from the same or a different data source by the Data Source View Designer feature of SQL Server 2008. When a table is replaced, all other objects in the SSAS database or project having references to the table continue to reference it because the object ID for the table in the data source view remains the same.

On the other hand, if the user deletes and then adds a table, all the references and relationships are lost and must be recreated. To replace a table with another table, the user must have an active connection to the source data in the Data Source View Designer in project mode.

Answer option C is incorrect. Deleting a table in a data source view will delete all other objects in the SSAS database or project that references it.

Answer option D is incorrect. There is no such command as ALTER_VIEW.

A16. Answer option C is correct.

The Raw File Source is used to store the native SSIS data in a binary file which is useful for data staging.

Answer option A is incorrect. The Excel Source allows extractions from an Excel worksheet which are defined in an Excel file.

Answer option B is incorrect. The OLE DB Source is used to make a connection to the installed OLE DB providers, such as SQL Server, Access, SSAS, and Oracle.

Answer option D is incorrect. The XML Source allows raw data to be extracted from an XML file. It also requires an XML schema to define data associations.

A17. Answer option A is correct.

The DMX query designer is used to retrieve data from a data mining model. A user should have an Analysis Services data source that includes a data mining model if he wants to use the DMX query designer. After the model is selected, data mining prediction queries can be created that provides data to a report.

Answer option B is incorrect. The MDX query designer is used for creating queries that run against an Analysis Services or other multidimensional data source. The MDX query designer becomes available when a dataset is created in Report Designer that uses SAP NetWeaver BI data source or Analysis Services.

Answer option C is incorrect. The generic query designer is the default query building tool for most supported relational data sources, including Oracle, OLE DB, XML Web services, Microsoft SQL Server, and ODBC. In contrast with the graphical query designer, query syntax is not validated during query design by the generic query designer tool. This query designer is recommended for creating complex queries, stored procedures, for writing dynamic queries, and for querying XML data.

Answer option D is incorrect. The graphical query designer is a query design tool that is used in other SQL Server components and in several Microsoft products. It provides a visual design environment for selecting columns and tables. It builds the Transact-SQL statements and joins for a user automatically when he selects which columns to use.

Answer option E is incorrect. The Report Model query designer is used to modify or create queries that run against a report model that has been published to a report server. Clickthrough data exploration is supported by the reports that run against models. The path of data exploration is determined by the query at run time. In order to use the Report Model query designer, data source that points to a published model should be defined. The Report Model query designer can be used in either graphical or generic mode.

A18. Answer option A is correct.

The association rules algorithm is a data mining algorithm that is designed for market basket analysis. It defines an item set as a combination of items in a single transaction. The algorithm scans the dataset and counts the number of times item sets appear in transactions.

Answer option B is incorrect. The Naive Bayes algorithm calculates probabilities for each possible state of the input attribute. The user can later use those probabilities to predict an outcome of the target attribute based on the known input attributes. Because this algorithm is quite simple, it builds the models very quickly. Thus, it can be used as a starting point in prediction tasks. This algorithm does not support continuous attributes.

Answer option C is incorrect. The clustering algorithm is a segmentation algorithm provided by SQL Server 2008 Analysis Services (SSAS). This is an iterative algorithm that groups cases in a dataset into clusters with similar characteristics. These groupings are useful for exploring data, identifying anomalies in the data, and creating predictions.

For example, consider a group of people who share similar demographic information and who buy similar products from the Adventure Works company. This group of people represents a cluster of data. Several such clusters may exist in a database. By observing the columns that make up a cluster, one can more clearly see how records in a dataset are related to one another.

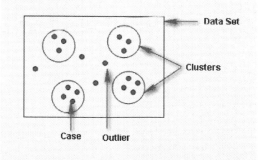

Answer option D is incorrect. The Decision Trees algorithm is the most popular data mining algorithm, which is used to predict discrete and continuous variables. The reason that this algorithm is so popular is that the results generated are very easy to understand by the user. If a user predicts continuous variables, he gets piecewise multiple linear regression formulae with separate formulae in each node of a tree. The discrete input variables are used by the algorithm to split the tree into nodes. A tree that predicts continuous variables is a Regression Tree.

A19. Answer option A is correct.

The CLUSTERING_METHOD parameter of the clustering algorithm specifies the clustering method for the algorithm (the K-Means algorithm and the Expectation Maximization (EM) method) to use. The following clustering methods are available:

ID	Method
1	Scalable EM
2	Non-scalable EM
3	Scalable K-Means
4	Non-scalable K-Means

Note: The default is 1 (scalable EM).

Answer option B is incorrect. The MODELLING_CARDINALITY parameter of the Clustering algorithm is used to specify the number of sample models that are constructed during the clustering process. If the number of candidate models is reduced, it may improve the performance at the risk of missing some good quality models. The default value of this parameter is 10.

Answer option C is incorrect. The CLUSTER_COUNT parameter is used to specify the approximate number of clusters that a clustering algorithm should build. The algorithm builds as many clusters as possible if the approximate number of clusters cannot be built from the data. The default value of CLUSTER_COUNT is 10. If the value is set to 0, it causes the algorithm to use heuristic to determine the number of clusters to build.

Answer option D is incorrect. The STOPPING_TOLERANCE parameter of the Clustering algorithm specifies the value that is used to find out when convergence is attained and when the algorithm has finished building the model. When the overall change in cluster probabilities is less than the ratio of the STOPPING_TOLERANCE parameter divided by the size of the model, the convergence is reached. The default value of this parameter is 10.

Answer option E is incorrect. The SAMPLE_SIZE parameter of the clustering algorithm specifies the number of cases that is used by the algorithm on each pass if the parameter of the CLUSTERING_METHOD is set to one of the scalable clustering methods. If the SAMPLE_SIZE parameter is set to 0, it will cause the whole dataset to be clustered in a single pass, which may cause memory and performance issue. The default value of the SAMPLE_SIZE is 50000.

A20.   Answer option A is correct.

The Naive Bayes data mining algorithm is used to calculate the probabilities for each possible state of the input attribute, provided that each state of the predictable attribute is given. These probabilities can be used later to predict an outcome of the target attribute that a user is predicting, based on the known input attributes. This algorithm is very simple and is capable of building the models very quickly. Therefore, this algorithm can be used by users as a starting point in their prediction task. The Naive Bayes algorithm does not support continuous attributes.

Answer option B is incorrect. The Decision Trees algorithm is the most popular data mining algorithm, which is used to predict discrete and continuous variables. The reason that this algorithm is so popular is that the results generated are very easy to understand by the user. If a user predicts continuous variables, he gets piecewise multiple linear regression formulae with separate formulae in each node of a tree. The discrete input variables are used by the algorithm to split the tree into nodes. A tree that predicts continuous variables is a Regression Tree.

Answer option C is incorrect. The Association Rules data mining algorithm is designed for the market basket analysis. The algorithm defines an itemset as a combination of items in a single transaction. The algorithm scans the dataset and counts the number of times the itemsets appear in the transactions. This algorithm should be used for detecting the cross-selling opportunities.

Answer option D is incorrect. The Clustering Algorithm is used to group cases from a dataset into a cluster containing similar characteristics. With the help of these cluster, the users can explore the data and learn about relationships among their cases.

Additionally, a user can create predictions from the clustering model created by the algorithm.

A21.   Answer option C is correct.

SQL Server Browser service is a tool used to connect to an SQL Server instance if a DBA is not able to connect to that instance through DAC. It can be configured either during the installation of SQL Server or by using the Surface Area Configuration Manager tool. This service starts automatically by default. It listens to incoming requests and connects to the correct instance. It also displays a list of all available instances on the server and connects to DAC endpoints. The SQL Server Browser service automatically listens on port 1434 for connections to any instance of SQL Server 2008 running on a server when it has been configured to automatically start. SQL clients will normally connect using port 1434 and the SQL Server Browser service will handle the request.

Answer option A is incorrect. If the SQL Server Browser service is not running, users must include port 1433 in the connection query to connect to the default instance. Opening port 1434 won't change the client's connection query.

Answer option B is incorrect. If the SQL Server Browser service is not running, users must include port 1433 in the connection query to connect to the default instance. Opening ports 1433 and/or 1434 won't change the client's connection query.

Answer option D is incorrect. The SQL Server Agent service is used for maintenance and management tasks. It is not needed for connectivity. SQL Server Agent is used to automate administrative tasks. It is used to add jobs, store job information, run a job on a schedule, etc. By default, it is disabled at the time of installation. To enable this tool, a user has to explicitly start it.

A22.   Answer option A is correct.

The sys.dm_exec_query_stats dynamic management view can provide a significant amount of detail on cached queries. Each query is cached before it is run and queries that are frequently run will stay in cache much longer than single queries. As an example, the following query returns information about the top five queries ranked by average CPU time. This example aggregates the queries according to their query hash, so that logically equivalent queries are grouped by their cumulative resource consumption.

USE Exams;

GO

SELECT TOP 5 query_stats.query_hash AS "Query Hash",

SUM(query_stats.total_worker_time)   /
SUM(query_stats.execution_count)

While not mentioned, SQL Profiler would also be an ideal solution to create a trace to track and log query performance.

Answer option B is incorrect. While a query using a query hint is very likely not using the least amount of resources, simply looking for a query that uses query hints doesn't tell you that it's using the most CPU time. Still, as a general rule, SQL Server can perform better without query hints than it will with them. If query hints are located, you often can delete them and achieve better performance.

Answer option C is incorrect. SQL Server Agent is used to automate administrative tasks. It is used to add jobs, store job information, run a job on a schedule, etc. By default, it is disabled at the time of installation. To enable this tool, a user has to explicitly start it. SQL Server Agent is designed to create jobs. It isn't designed to track and log CPU time for queries.

Answer option D is incorrect. SSRS stands for SQL Server Reporting Services. It creates and manages Web-enabled reporting services. It is used to create and generate reports, to retrieve data from various data sources, and to publish reports in various formats. SQL Server Reporting Services (SSRS) doesn't have traces that can be enabled. SQL Profiler could be used to create traces.

A23.   Answer option A is correct.

You will create a data source view that is associated with the "CustCont" and "Cust" datasources and add the tables to the data source view. A data source view is a document that is used to describe the schema of an underlying data source. It provides destinations and lookup tables for SQL Server Integration Services tasks, transformations, data sources, and destinations. A data source view is built on a data source. A data source view, in Integration Services, is a design-time object that makes it simple to implement the same data source in multiple packages. It is also possible to extend a data source view. Data source views can be created in Business Intelligence Development Studio, Analysis Services, and in Integration Services projects.

The snowflake schema is used in the data warehouse applications and is basically an extended StarSchema where each point of the star branches to more points. In the snowflake schema, the star schema dimension tables are more controlled.

The advantages of the snowflake schema are as follows:

Improved query performance due to minimized disk storage for the data.

Improved performance by joining smaller normalized tables, rather than large denormalized ones.

The snowflake schema also increases the flexibility of the application because the normalization lowers the granularity of the dimensions. However, since the snowflake schema has more tables, it also increases the complexities of some of the queries that need to be mapped.

Answer options B, C, and D are incorrect. As explained in answer option A, these ways do not satisfy the conditions for a snowflake schema.

A24.   Answer option C is correct.

You should add a matrix template to accomplish the task. The matrix template is used to display aggregated data summaries which are grouped in rows and columns, analogous to a PivotTable or a crosstab. The number of rows and columns for groups can be calculated by the number of unique values for each row and column groups.

Answer option A is incorrect. A subreport is similar to a frame in a Web page. A subreport is a report that displays another report inside the body of a main report. In other words, it is used to embed another report within a report. Any report can be used as a subreport. The subreport can use different data sources than the main report. Subreports are typically used within a main report as a briefing book or as a container for a collection of related reports.

Answer options B and D are incorrect. The textbox and rectangle data regions cannot fulfill the third requirement. The Tablix data region is a universal layout report item that displays report data in cells which are ordered in the form of rows and columns. Report data can be detail data, as it is taken from the data source, or aggregated detail data arranged into groups which are specified by the user. Each Tablix cell can include any report item, such as a text box, or an image.

The table, matrix, and list data regions are represented in the toolbox by templates for the fundamental Tablix data region. When the user adds one of these templates to a report, he is essentially adding a Tablix data region that is optimized for a particular data layout. As groups for a table, matrix, or list are defined by the user, the Report Designer adds rows and columns to the Tablix data region.

A25. Answer option D is correct.

The Business Intelligence Development Studio feature is used to install the tools for designing packages in SQL Server 2008. BIDS, the 32-bit development environment for Integration Services packages, is not supported on the Itanium 64-bit operating system and is not installed on Itanium servers.

Answer option A is incorrect. The Client Tools Backward Compatibility feature is used to install the Execute DTS 2000 Package task if the support for DTS packages is required.

Answer option B is incorrect. The configuration file is needed to be modified if you have to manage packages that are stored in a named instance or a remote instance of the Database Engine, or in multiple instances of the Database Engine.

Answer option C is incorrect. The registry key that specifies the package location is needed to be modified if you move the configuration file to a location other than its default location.

A26. Answer options A and B are correct.

The Package Migration Wizard can be started with the help of either Business Intelligence Development Studio (BIDS) or SQL Server Management Studio (SSMS).

BIDS: When using BIDS, a user should first navigate to the Solution Explorer, right-click the SSIS packages folder, and then select Migrate DTS 2000 Package.

SSMS: When using SSMS, a user should first connect to an SQL Server 2008 instance. In the Object Explorer, he should open the Management/Legacy folder, select the Data Transformation folder, and then select Migrate Package.

Answer option C is incorrect. Online analytical processing, or OLAP, is an approach to quickly answer multi-dimensional analytical queries. OLAP is part of the broader category of business intelligence, which also encompasses relational reporting and data mining. The typical applications of OLAP are in business reporting for sales, marketing, management reporting, business process management (BPM), budgeting and forecasting, financial reporting, and similar areas.

Databases configured for OLAP use a multidimensional data model, allowing for complex analytical and ad-hoc queries with a rapid execution time. They borrow aspects of navigational databases and hierarchical databases that are faster than relational databases.

The output of an OLAP query is typically displayed in a matrix (or pivot) format. The dimensions form the rows and columns of the matrix; the measures form the values.

Answer option D is incorrect. A data source view is a document that is used to describe the schema of an underlying data source. It provides destinations and lookup tables for SQL Server Integration Services tasks, transformations, data sources, and destinations. A data source view is built on a data source. A data source view, in Integration Services, is a design-time object that makes it simple to implement the same data source in multiple packages. It is also possible to extend a data source view. Data source views can be created in Business Intelligence Development Studio, Analysis Services, and in Integration Services projects.

A27.   Answer options B and D are correct.

If changes are frequent, under the full recovery model settings, frequent log backups should be scheduled.

If changes are frequent, under the full recovery model settings, scheduling differential backups between full backups reduces restore time by reducing the number of log backups you have to restore after restoring the data.

Answer option A is incorrect. Under the full recovery model, scheduling differential backups before and after full database backups does not provide any benefit for data backup and restoration.

Answer option C is incorrect. Partial backups are designed for use under the simple recovery model, not under the full recovery model.

A28.   Answer option B is correct.

A staging area is a place to hold temporary tables on a data warehouse server. The staging area is mostly needed to hold the data, and to carry out data cleansing and merging, before loading the data into the warehouse. Having a staging area decouples the extraction processes from operational processes. This serves to reduce the load placed on the source systems by the extraction processes. Moreover, using staging areas allows multiple source systems to increase performance which can act as an integration point prior to the processing of transformations.

Answer option A is incorrect. Collecting data directly from the operational sources and integrating it will not improve performance.

Answer option C is incorrect. The OPENROWSET function in Transact-SQL can be used to pass a connection string and query to a data source to retrieve the required data. If this function is used to retrieve the data from a SQL Server instance, then that instance must be configured to permit ad hoc distributed queries.

The OPENROWSET function can be referenced in the FROM clause of a query as if it were a table name. This function can also be referenced as the target table of an INSERT, UPDATE, or DELETE statement, subject to the capabilities of the OLE DB provider. Although the query might return multiple result sets, OPENROWSET returns only the first one.

Answer option D is incorrect. A linked server configuration facilitates SQL Server to execute commands against OLE DB data sources on remote servers. Linked servers offer the following advantages:

- Access to Remote server.

- The capacity to issue distributed queries, updates, commands, and transactions on heterogeneous data sources across the enterprise.

- The capacity to address diverse data sources likewise.

A29.   Answer option B is correct.

The geometry data type is used to store planar spatial data and perform operations on it. The geometry data type is a type of spatial data type which is used to store planar (flat-earth) data in SQL Server 2008. It is generally used to store XY coordinates that represent points, lines, and polygons in a two-dimensional space.

The geometry data type supports a flat 2D surface with XY coordinates for representing points. Points can be on lines and can also mark the edges of polygons. There are methods like STintersects, STArea, STDistance, STTouch, etc. which assist the geometry data type. For example, storing XY coordinates in the geometry data type can be used to map the exterior of a building.

Answer option A is incorrect. The geography data type is used to store geodetic spatial data and perform operations on it.

Answer option C is incorrect. In SQL Server 2008, the hierarchyid data type has been added to store values that represent the position of nodes of a hierarchal tree structure.

Answer option D is incorrect. The filestream data type is used for storing unstructured data in the file system.

A30.   Answer option D is correct.

The filestream data type in SQL Server 2008 can be used to store unstructured data, such as videos, graphic files, Word documents, Excel spreadsheets, etc. Filestream is not a data type, but is a variant of the VARBINARY(MAX) data type which enables unstructured data to be stored in the file system instead of being stored in the SQL Server database.

Answer option A is incorrect. The date and time data type is used to keep track of the date and time zones. SQL Server 2008 introduces four new date and time data types, which include:

- DATE: The DATE data type stores a date in the format of YYYY-MM-DD. It has a range of 0001-01-01 through 9999-12-32, which should be adequate for most business and scientific applications.

- TIME: The TIME data type stores time in the format of hh:mm:ss.nnnnnnn, with a range of 00:00:00.0000000 through 23:59:59:9999999 and is accurate to 100 nanoseconds.

- DATETIME2: The DATETIME2 has a greater range and precision than the older DATETIME data type. The format of date and time is YYYY-MM-DD hh:mm:ss:nnnnnnnm with a range of 0001-01-01 00:00:00.0000000 through 9999-12-31 23:59:59.9999999, and an accuracy of 100 nanoseconds.

- DATETIMEOFFSET: The DATETIMEOFFSET is similar to the DATETIME2 data type, but it includes additional information to track the time zone. The format of the time zone is YYYY-MM-DD hh:mm:ss[.nnnnnnn] [+|-]hh:mm with a range of 0001-01-01 00:00:00.0000000 through 9999-12-31 23:59:59.9999999, and an accuracy of 100 nanoseconds.

All of these new date and time data types work with SQL Server 2008 date and time functions, which have been improved to understand the new formats accurately.

Answer option B is incorrect. The hierarchyid data type is used to enable database applications to model hierarchical tree structures, such as the organization chart of a business. It is designed to store values that represent the position of nodes of a hierarchal tree structure. For example, the hierarchyid data type makes it simple to represent these types of relationships without the need of multiple parent/child tables and complex joins.

As compared to the standard data types, the hierarchyid data type is a CLR user-defined type providing various methods to manipulate the date stored within it. The hierarchyid data type is used to store hierarchical data; it does not automatically represent a hierarchical structure. A hierarchyid data type can be considered as a place to store positional nodes of a tree structure, not as a way to create the tree structure.

Answer option C is incorrect. Spatial data types were introduced in SQL Server 2008 to store spatial information. These are of two types as follows:

- Geometry data type

- Geography data type

A31.   Answer option A is correct.

The DelayValidation property gets or sets a Boolean that indicates whether validation of the task is delayed until run time. Its value should be set to true if validation of the package is delayed until run time. Its value is false if the package is validated, and warnings and errors are returned before the package is actually executed. False is the default value and may prevent the package from running if warnings or errors occur that exceed the MaximumErrorCount property.

Answer option B is incorrect. The FailPackageOnFailure property is used to set or get a Boolean that indicates whether the package fails when the child container fails. If FailPackageOnFailure property is true and the execution result of a container is a failure, the execution result assigned to the package that is the parent of the failed container is also a failure. This results in the termination of the package. This event gives the definition of the restartable packge failure. Those packages, which are unable to complete, cannot be started because their execution was cancelled.

Note: The FailPackageOnFailure property cannot be set on package. If this property is set to true on the package, it will result in an error.

Answer option C is incorrect. The SuspendRequired property gets or sets a Boolean that indicates if tasks should suspend when they encounter a breakpoint. This value is set by the runtime engine for containers and tasks when a breakpoint is encountered. Its value is true if the task suspends when it encounters a breakpoint.

Answer option D is incorrect. There is no such property as NoDestination

A32.   Answer option B is correct.

The lookup in Partial Caching mode searches the cache for a query match. If a match is not found, then a query against the data source will be executed and the pipeline row is redirected as configured. If a match is found, it is held in the cache.

Answer option A is incorrect. This is the feature of lookup in No Caching mode.

Answer options C and D are incorrect. These are the features of lookup in Full Caching mode.

A33.   Answer option A is correct.

You should choose the Scheduled MOLAP storage setting to accomplish the task. In Scheduled MOLAP, detail data and aggregations are stored in a multidimensional format. Notification is not received by the server when the data changes, and processing automatically occurs every 24 hours. This setting is normally used for a data source when there is requirement of only daily updates. In the MOLAP cache, queries are always against data that is not discarded until a new cache is built and its objects are processed.

Answer option B is incorrect. In Medium Latency MOLAP, detail data and aggregations are stored in multidimensional format. While MOLAP objects are reprocessed in a cache, the server listens for notifications of changes to the data and switches to real-time ROLAP. A silence interval of around 10 seconds is required before the cache is updated. If the silence interval is not attained, there is an override interval of 10 minutes. As data changes, processing occurs automatically with a target latency of four hours.

This setting is usually used for a data source that has frequent or less frequent updates and when query performance is more important than always providing the most current data. This setting processes MOLAP objects automatically whenever required after the latency interval. Performance is slower while the MOLAP objects are being reprocessed.

Answer option C is incorrect. In Automatic MOLAP, detail data and aggregations are stored in multidimensional format. The server listens for notifications and retains the current MOLAP cache while it builds a new one. The server never switches to real-time OLAP, and while the new cache is built, the queries may be stale. A silence interval of around 10 seconds is required before the creation of a new MOLAP cache. If the silence interval is not attained, there is an override interval of 10 minutes. Processing occurs automatically as data changes with a target latency of two hours.

This setting is typically used for a data source when the performance of the query is of prime importance. MOLAP objects are processed automatically by this setting, whenever required, after the latency interval. The most recent data is not returned by the queries while the new cache is being built and processed.

Answer option D is incorrect. In Low Latency MOLAP, detail data and aggregations are stored in multidimensional format. While MOLAP objects are reprocessed in a cache, the server listens for notifications of changes to the data and switches to real-time ROLAP. A silence interval of around 10 seconds is required before the cache is updated. If the silence interval is not attained, there is an override interval of 10 minutes. As data changes, processing occurs automatically with a target latency of 30 minutes after the first change.

This setting is usually used for a data source that has frequent updates and when query performance is more important than always providing the most current data. This setting processes MOLAP objects automatically whenever required after the latency interval. Performance is slower while the MOLAP objects are being reprocessed.

A34. Answer option A is correct.

The Process Structure option for OLAP (Online Analytical Processing) objects is used to delete the partition data and apply Process Default to the cube dimension?

The different processing options for OLAP objects are described in the following table:

Processing Options	Description
Process Default	It is used to perform the minimum number of tasks required to fully initialize the object. Based on the object state, this option is converted by the server to one of the other options.
Process Update	It is used to apply member inserts, updates, and deletes without invalidating the affected cubes.
Process Full	It used to drop the object stores and rebuild the object. It is also used to perform the meta-data changes, such as adding a new

attribute to a dimension.

Process Add	It is used to add new data.
Process Index	It is used to retain data and for building only the aggregations and indexes.
Process Data	It is used to load the object with data without building aggregations and indexes.
Unprocess	It is used to delete the object data or the data in the containing objects.
Process Structure	It is used to delete the partition data. It also applies Process Default to the cube dimensions.

A35. Answer option A is correct.

The low-latency MOLAP is used for a data source that has frequent updates and when query performance is more important than always providing the most current data. Creating a partition for each month and setting the storage setting of the partition for the current month to low-latency multidimensional online analytical processing will improve the cube processing and also the query response time.

Answer options B, C, and D are incorrect. These tasks will not decrease the cube processing time and the query response time.

A36. Answer option A is correct.

The syntax of a default Report Manager URL for a named instance is http://[ComputerName]/Reports_[InstanceName]. Since the computer name for SQL Server 2008 is SQL1 and the name of the second instance of Reporting services is Inst1, the correct syntax should be http://[SQL1]/Reports_[Inst1].

Answer option B is incorrect. The http:// [ComputerName]/Reports URL is used when the default setting of the Report Server is used. Since the default instance does not have a name, it is referenced with the help of the Computer name in which the Reporting Services is installed.

Answer options C and D are incorrect. These options are syntactically incorrect.

A37. Answer options A, B, and C are correct.

SQL Server 2008 Integration Services (SSIS) provides the following three types of control flow elements:

Containers: Containers are used to provide structure in packages and services to tasks in the control flow. Following are the different types of containers in the Integration Services for grouping tasks and implementing repeating control flows:

- Foreach Loop container: This container enumerates a collection and repeats its control flow for each member of the collection.

- For Loop container: This container repeats its control flow until a specified expression evaluates to False.

- Sequence container: This container allows a user to define a subset of the control flow within a container and to manage container and tasks as a unit.

- Tasks: An SQL Server 2005/2008 Integration Services (SSIS) package is made up of one or more tasks. If more than one task is present in the package, they are connected and sequenced by precedence constraints in the control flow. Tasks are control flow elements that define units of work that are performed in a package control flow.

The custom tasks can also be written by using a programming language that supports a .NET programming language, such as C#, or COM, such as Visual Basic. The SSIS Designer provides the design surface for creating package control flow, and provides custom editors for configuring tasks.

Precedence constraints: The order that tasks are executed is controlled by precedence constraints. If a user wants to change the order of precedence, he must delete and recreate a precedence constraint. Once a precedence constraint is created, the user can modify the value and define how multiple constraints can work together using logical AND and logical OR statements. However, the precedence order cannot be modified.

Answer option D is incorrect. SQL Server Integration Services transformations are the components in the data flow of a package that merge, aggregate, distribute, and modify data. Lookup operations and sample datasets generation can also be performed with the help of transformations. The different types of transformations included in SQL Server Integration Services are as follows:

- Row Transformations

- Rowset Transformations

- Auditing Transformations

- Custom Transformations

- Split and Join Transformations

- Business Intelligence Transformations

A38.   Answer options B, C, and E are correct.

As mentioned in the question, you want the package to use a single transaction for all the tasks (Data Flow tasks and Control Flow tasks). When using a single transaction option for configuring the package, the package itself initiates a single transaction. You should configure the package to initiate that transaction by setting the TransactionOption property of the package to Required.

After this, you want to enlist the three Data Flow tasks and three Control Flow tasks into that single transaction. To enlist a task in a transaction, you should set the TransactionOption property of all the Data Flow tasks and Control Flow tasks to Supported.

A39.   Answer option A is correct.

The Progress tab of the SSIS Designer is used to view the progress of the execution of an Integration Services package. The Progress tab lists the start time, the elapsed time, and the finish time for the validation and execution of the package and its executables. This tab also displays any information or warnings for the package, success or failure of the package, progress notifications, and any error message that are generated during the execution of the package. The Progress tab becomes the Execution Results tab after the package stops running.

Answer option B is incorrect. The OnProgress event handler is the event handler for the OnError event. This event is raised by an executable when an error occurs. Since you want to capture only the start, finish, and elapsed time of the package execution, the OnProgress event handler should not be enabled to accomplish the task.

Answer option C is incorrect. It is possible to capture the start, finish, and elapsed time for the validation and execution of the package.

Answer option D is incorrect. Checkpoints work together with transactions to enable package restartability. The unit of work that needs to be completed successfully in order for the data to be applied is called transaction. In the SQL Server Integration Services (SSIS) instead of running the whole package, failed packages can be started from the point of failure called checkpoints. Information about the packages execution is written to the checkpoint file only if a package is configured to use the checkpoints. This checkpoint file is used to restart the package from the point of failure when the failed package is rerun. The checkpoint file gets deleted if the package runs successfully, and then recreated the next time when the package runs.

A40.   Answer options A, B, and C are correct.

Transactions in SSIS use the Microsoft Distributed Transaction Coordinator (MSDTC). This service should be started on the computer for a transaction to work. Any service or program that is enabled to work with the MSDTC can be part of a transaction in SSIS.

It is mentioned in the question that a series of tasks must be completed as a single unit in which either all the tasks are successful and committed or an error is generated and none of the tasks are committed. Therefore, you should place the task within a Sequence Container and then set the TransactionOption property of the container to Required.

Answer option D is incorrect. When the TransactionOption property of the container is set to Supported, a task can inherit the transaction setting of its parent. This is the default setting when a task or a container is created.

Answer option E is incorrect. A task can be prevented from participating in a transaction by setting its TransactionOption property to NotSupported.

A41.   Answer option C is correct.

An FTP connection manager allows a package to make a connection to a File Transfer Protocol (FTP) server. The FTP task included in SQL Server Integration Services makes use of this connection manager.

When an FTP connection manager is added to a package, Integration Services creates a connection manager that can be resolved as an FTP connection at run time, sets the connection manager properties, and adds the connection manager to the Connections collection on the package.

Answer option A is incorrect. The Fullpath in FTP connection can be specified via expressions.

Answer option B is incorrect. The FTP service supports static as well as dynamic variables.

Answer option D is incorrect. The package scope is correct.

A42.   Answer options A, B, and D are correct.

There are three primary containers in SSIS, which are as follows:

- Sequence Container: It organizes the subsidiary tasks by grouping them together and lets a user apply transactions or allocate logging to the container.

- For Loop Container: It provides the same functionality as the Sequence Container except that it also allows a user to run the tasks within it multiple times based on an evaluation condition, such as looping from 1 to 10.

- Foreach Loop Container: It allows looping, but instead of providing a condition expression, it loops over a set of objects such as files in a folder.

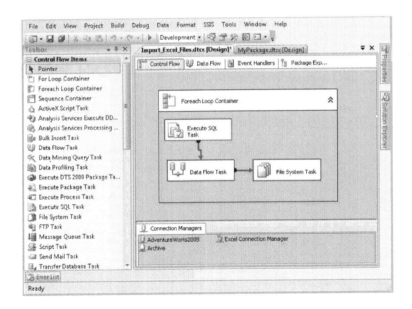

Note: Additionally, the user can drag task objects and other containers into his container.

Answer options C and E are incorrect. There are no such primary containers in SSIS 2008.

A43.   Answer option A is correct.

The Usage-Based Optimization Wizard is used to design aggregations for a partition. This wizard is very useful for designing aggregations based on the specific usage patterns of queries recorded in the query log of an Analysis Services instance. The Usage-Based Optimization Wizard is similar in output to the Aggregation Design Wizard.

Aggregations are pre-calculated summaries of data from leaf cells. They are very efficient in reducing the query execution time and improving query response time by preparing the answers before the questions are asked. Aggregations are used to provide performance improvements by allowing Microsoft SQL Server Analysis Services (SSAS) to retrieve pre-calculated totals directly from cube storage instead of recalculating data from an underlying data source for each query.

Answer option B is incorrect. The Cube Wizard is not used to design aggregations. The Cube Wizard is used to create a cube for a Microsoft SQL Server Analysis Services (SSAS) project in Business Intelligence Development Studio. To open this wizard in Business Intelligence Development Studio in Solution Explorer, right-click the Cubes folder for an Analysis Services project, and then click New Cube. After the Cube Wizard has been created, its properties can be modified by the Cube Designer in Business Intelligence Development Studio (BIDS).

Answer option C is incorrect. Although SQL Profiler is used to identify slow running queries, it cannot be used to examine the execution plans to analyze and design aggregations. SQL Server Profiler is a tool used to monitor and trace events. The events generated can be used to find the slow running queries and to determine the cause of a deadlock and that of slow running queries. The events that are captured by SQL Server Profiler are as follows:

- Login connections, failures, and disconnections

- Transact-SQL statements

- Remote procedure call

- The start or end of a stored procedure and statements within it

- The start or end of a transact-SQL batch

- An error written to the SQL Server error log

- Locks and deadlocks

Answer option D is incorrect. It is possible to identify slow running queries by analyzing aggregations.

A44.   Answer option A is correct.

The different cube designer tabs are described in the following table:

Tab Name	Description
Cube Structure	It is used to edit the primary structure of a cube.
Calculations	It contains MDX formulas and scripts to define named sets and calculated members.
Dimension Usage	It is used to define the relationship between the dimensions and measure groups within the cube.
KPIs	It is used to define key performance indicators within the cube. It includes formulas for KPI status and trends.
Actions	It is used to create actions, such as running reports or launching URLs, that will be available to end users as they browse the cube.
Perspectives	It is used to create subsets of the cube content for easier browsing at the end-user side.
Partitions	It is used to define the storage used for each measure groups within a cube.
Translations	It is used to define language translations for a cube's metadata, like dimension names, measure named, etc.

A45.   Answer options A and B are correct.

In order to configure the default storage settings for new measure groups added to a cube, you should take the following two steps:

On the Cube Builder tab in the Cube Wizard, click the cube object in either the Measures or Dimensions pane.

In the Properties window, click the browse (...) button for the ProactiveCaching property setting.

Answer option C is incorrect. In order to configure the default storage settings for the new partitions added to a measure group, you should expand the measure group on the Partitions tab in the Cube Wizard and click the Storage Settings link for that measure group.

Answer option D is incorrect. If you want to configure storage for an existing partition, you should expand the measure group on the Partitions tab in the Cube Wizard. After this, you should right-click the partition, and then click Storage Settings.

A46. Answer option B is correct.

You should use the Log\QueryLog\QueryLogSampling property to accomplish the task. The different SSAS Server Logging Properties are described in the following table:

Option	Description
Log\Query\CreateQuery-LogTable	This property is set to true if a user needs that the table should be created by the QueryLog operation.
Log\QueryLog\QueryLogSampling	This property defines how frequently queries are captured. This property has 10 as its default value, which means that only 1 of every 10 queries is captured. This reduces overhead.
Log\QueryLog\QueryLog-ConnectionString	This property uses the general Connection Manager to define a connection string to the server and database, which will capture the

log table.

| Log\QueryLog\ TableName | QueryLog- | This property is used to define the query name to which the queries will be captured. |

A47. Answer option A is correct.

The Parallel processing setting is used for batch processing. This setting causes Analysis Services to fork off processing tasks to execute in parallel inside a single transaction. If a failure occurs, the result generated is a rollback of all changes. A user can set the maximum number of parallel tasks, or allow the server to decide the optimal distribution. The Parallel processing option is useful for speeding up the processing.

Answer option B is incorrect. The Sequential (Transaction mode) processing setting is used to control the execution of the processing job. Following are the two options available:

- One Transaction: If this option is selected, the processing job runs as a transaction. All the changes by the processing job are committed if all the processes inside the processing job succeed. If any of the processes fails, all the changes by the processing job are rolled back. One Transaction is the default value.

- Separate Transactions: If this option is selected, each process in the processing job runs as a stand-alone job. If any one process fails, only that process is rolled back and the processing job continues. Each job commits all process changes at the end of the job.

Answer option C is incorrect. The Writeback Table processing setting is used to control the handling of writeback tables during processing. This setting is applied to writeback partitions in a cube, and it uses the following three options:

- Use Existing: It uses the existing writeback table. It is the default value.

- Create: It is used to create a new writeback table and causes the process to fail if one already exists.

- Create Always: It is used to create a new writeback table even if one already exists. If this is selected, then the existing table is deleted and replaced.

Answer option D is incorrect. There is no such processing setting as Default.

A48.   Answer option A is correct.

You should set the key not found option when a key value exists in a partition but does not exist in the corresponding dimension. Report and continue is the default setting. Report and stop and Ignore error are the other settings.

Answer option B is incorrect. Duplicate key is the error that occurs when more than one key value exists in a dimension. Ignore error is the default setting. Report and stop and Report and Continue are the other settings.

Answer option C is incorrect. Null key converted to unknown is the error that occurs when a key value is null and the Key error action is set to Convert to unknown. Ignore error is the default setting. Report and stop and Report and continue are the other settings.

Answer option D is incorrect. Null key not allowed is the error that occurs when Key error action is set to Discard record. Report and continue is the default setting. Other settings are Ignore error and Report and stop.

A49.   Answer options A and B are correct.

Dimensions in Microsoft SQL Server 2008 Analysis Services (SSAS) support two storage modes:

- Relational OLAP (ROLAP)

- Multidimensional OLAP (MOLAP)

ROLAP (Relational Online Analytical Processing) is the storage mode for the dimensions. The dimensions that uses ROLAP store the data in the tables that are used to define dimension. The ROLAP storage mode, at the expense of query performance, can support large dimensions without duplicating large amount of data. The ROLAP storage mode can also support real-time OLAP because the dimension relies directly on the tables in the data source view that is used to define the dimensions.

MOLAP (Multidimensional Online Analytical Processing) is the default storage mode for dimensions. The dimension that uses MOLAP stores its data in a multidimensional structure in the instance of Microsoft's SQL Server Analysis Services. This MOLAP is created and populated when the dimension is processed. The quality performance of MOLAP dimensions is better than ROLAP (Relational Online Analytical Processing) dimensions.

Answer option C is incorrect. HOLAP (Hybrid Online Analytical Processing) is a compromise between MOLAP (Multidimensional Online Analytical Processing) and ROLAP (Relational Online Analytical Processing). The storage of aggregates is done in the MOLAP file, while the base-level detail is kept in the data mart. This enhances the performance while browsing aggregates, but it slows down when a user "drills down" to base-level detail.

Answer option D is incorrect. Online analytical processing, or OLAP, is an approach to quickly answer multi-dimensional analytical queries. OLAP is part of the broader category of business intelligence, which also encompasses relational reporting and data mining. The typical applications of OLAP are in business reporting for sales, marketing, management reporting, business process management (BPM), budgeting and forecasting, financial reporting, and similar areas.

Databases configured for OLAP use a multidimensional data model, allowing for complex analytical and ad-hoc queries with a rapid execution time. They borrow aspects of navigational databases and hierarchical databases that are faster than relational databases.

The output of an OLAP query is typically displayed in a matrix (or pivot) format. The dimensions form the rows and columns of the matrix; the measures form the values.

A50. Answer options A and B are correct.

In order to add new cubes and dimensions to an SSAS solution, you can use either BIDS Cube Wizard or BIDS Dimension Wizard.

Answer option C is incorrect. The BIDS Cube Designer provides tabs for reviewing and modifying various aspects of a cube. The two tabs that are used to control the basic structure of a cube are the Dimension Usage tab and the Cube Structure tab.

Answer option D is incorrect. The BIDS Dimension Designer is used to modify a dimension and to add, delete, or modify specific attributes and multilevel hierarchies within the dimension.

Acronyms

CTE	Common table expression
DTC	Distributed Transaction Coordinator
SSA	SQL Server Agent
CLR	Common Language Runtime
AJAX	Asynchronouse Javascript and XML
CTE	Common table expressions
T-SQL	Transactional SQL
DR	Dirty read
2NF	Second normal form
4NF	Fourth normal form
DMCW	Database Mail Configuration Wizard
HPOM	High Protection operating mode
URI	Uniform Resource Identifier
RSB	Remote service binding
XPath	XML Path Language
DOM	Document Object Model
DML	Data Manipulation Language
DDL	Data Definition Language
DBA	Database administrator
CLR	Common Language Runtime
NF	Normal Form
ER-diagram	Entity Relationship diagram

WML	Wireless Markup Language
WSDL	Web Service Description Language
XAML	Yet Another Multicolumn Layout
XML	Extensible Markup Language
XSD	XML Schema Definition
DBMS	Database Management System
DLL	Dynamic Link Libraby
DOM	Document Object Model
HTML	Hyper Text Markup Language
HTTP	Hyper Text Trasnfer Protocol
HTTPS	Hypertext Transfer Protocol Secure
I/O	Input/Output
IIS	Internet Information Server
SOAP	Simple Object Access Protocol
SQL	Structured Query Language
SSL	Secure Socket Layer
UDDI	Universal Description, Discovery, and Integration
UI	User Interface
URI	Uniform Resource Identifier
URL	Uniform Resource Locator
UTC	Coordinated Universal Time
UTF	Unicode Transformation Format

Glossary

CLR table-valued functions

CLR table-valued functions return a table data-type. There is no function body for an inline table-valued function; the table is the result set of a single SELECT statement. The functionality of table-valued functions is extended by SQL Server just by allowing a user to define a table-valued function in any managed language. An IEnumerable or IEnumerator object returns the data from a table-valued function.

A CLR scalar-valued function returns only a single value, such as an integer, string, bit value, etc. These functions are accessible to T-SQL or other managed code. However, by using .NET Framework programming language users can create scalar-valued user-defined functions in managed code.

If a CLR assembly is not accessing any external resources, the permission set for the assembly should be SAFE. If CLR assemblies are signed, the TRUSTWORTHY database property can be kept OFF (False). CLR assemblies can be assigned permissions based on what is needed. For external resources that have been determined to be safe, EXTERNAL_ACCESS should be used.

CLR stored procedures

CLR stored procedures cannot be used in scalar expressions as they are routines and tabular messages. They can invoke data definition language and data manipulation language statements, as well return outputparameters. CLR stored procedures cannot be used in scalar expressions as they are routines and tabular messages.

Common table expression (CTE)

A common table expression (CTE) is a short-term result set that is defined within the implementation of a single INSERT, SELECT, DELETE, UPDATE, or CREATE VIEW statement. A CTE is similar to a derived table, i.e., it is not stored as an object and remains only for the duration of the query. A CTE can be self referencing and can be referenced multiple times in the same query not like a derived table.

Clustered index

A clustered index is organized as a B-tree structure. The index consists of a root page, intermediate levels, and leaf levels. The leaf level nodes contain the data pages of the underlying table. The root and intermediate level nodes contain index pages that hold index rows. Each index row contains a key value and a pointer.

Clustered and nonclustered index

There can be two types of indexes for a table: clustered and nonclustered. The difference between clustered and nonclustered indexes is that in clustered index, data itself is sorted in a particular order. While in a nonclustered index, data is stored in one place, index in another, with pointers to the storage location of data. Only one clustered index can be created per table. By default, clustered index is created for the primary key of the table. As the clustered index is a physical order of a table, table and clustered index cannot be separated and stored on different filegroups.

Check constraint

A check constraint is a condition that defines valid data when adding or updating an entry in a table of a relational database. A check constraint is applied to each row in the table. The constraint must be a predicate. It can refer to a single or multiple columns of the table. The result of the predicate can be either TRUE, FALSE, or UNKNOWN, depending on the presence of NULLs. If the predicate evaluates to UNKNOWN, then the constraint is not violated and the row can be inserted or updated in the table. This is contrary to the predicates in the WHERE clauses in the SELECT or UPDATE statements.

A database trigger executes implicitly when a triggering event such as a DML statement (INSERT, UPDATE, or DELETE) on a table, an INSTEAD OF trigger on a view, or a DDL statement (CREATE or ALTER) is issued, regardless of which database user is connected or which application is used. A database trigger also executes implicitly when some user actions or database system actions occur, e.g., when a database user logs on to the database or the database administrator (DBA) shuts down the database.

A database trigger can be a system trigger on a database or schema. A database trigger defined on a database fires for each event for all users. However, a database trigger defined on a schema fires for each event for that particular user.

A DML trigger is a database trigger whose triggering event is a Data Manipulation Language (DML) statement. A DML trigger has the following components:

Trigger timing: It decides the time of the trigger's execution in relation to the triggering event. Possible values are BEFORE, AFTER, and INSTEAD OF. BEFORE specifies that the trigger body will be executed before the triggering event is executed on the associated table. AFTER specifies that the trigger body will be executed after the triggering event is executed on the associated table. INSTEAD OF specifies that the trigger body will be executed instead of the triggering event. INSTEAD OF can be specified only for views and not for tables.

Triggering event: It specifies the Data Manipulation Language (DML) statement that causes the trigger to fire. Possible values are INSERT, UPDATE, and DELETE.

Trigger type: It determines how many times the trigger body executes. Possible values are statement (default) and row (FOR EACH ROW). Statement specifies that the trigger body will be executed only once for the triggering event, regardless of the number of rows affected by the triggering event. Row specifies that the trigger body will be executed once for each row affected by the triggering event.

Trigger body: It determines the action that the trigger will perform when it is fired. The trigger body is a complete PL/SQL block or a CALL statement that calls a stored procedure.

The syntax for creating a trigger is:

CREATE [OR REPLACE} TRIGGER trig_name

{BEFORE | AFTER | INSTEAD OF} event

ON {table_or_view_name | DATABASE]

[FOR EACH ROW [WHEN condition]]

trig_body;

FORCESEEK hint

The FORCESEEK hint can be used to force the query optimizer to perform an index seek operation. The FORCESEEK clause is included in the JOIN statement as shown in the following query:

SELECT*FROMOrdcrs AS o INNER JOIN OrderDetails AS d WITH (FORCESEEK) ON o.OrderID = d.OrderID

Geography data type

The geography data type is used to hold spatial data. Geography is a .NET common language runtime (CLR) data type that can store ellipsoidal (round-earth) data such as GPS latitude and longitude coordinates.

The geometry data type is a planar spatial data type that is implemented as a common language runtime (CLR) data type in SQL Server. This type represents data in a Euclidean (flat) coordinate system.

The data type that is used to store spatial data is known as spatial data type.

The two spatial data types supported by SQL Server 2008 are as follows:

1. GEOMETRY: It supports the geometric data based on the Euclidean coordinate system to store the points, lines, and polygons.

2. GEOGRAPHY: It denotes geographic objects on an area on the Earth's surface. The geographic data is mapped to a two-dimensional, non-Euclidean space by a spatial index specified on a geography column.

3. Understand some of the different data types used to express dates including the offsetdata type which includes the UTC offset. The geometry data type can hold latitude and longitude data used by GPS systems. Filestream data should be used for files larger than 1 MB that you want to store in the file system. Filestream data must be of the varbinary(max) data type. A HIERARCHYID data type is a new data type introduced in SQL Server 2008. It is a system-supplied CLR (Common language runtime) UDT (user defined type) that may be used for the manipulation and storage of the hierarchies.The varchar(max), varbinary(max), and xml data types can be used to display the data/reports from the database in xml format.

High Protection operating mode

High Protection operating mode, just like High Performance operating mode, does not have a witness server as part of the mirroring session. The transactions are transferred synchronously between the principal database and the mirror database. As the witness server is absent, the principal database does not form a quorum with the database. Automatic failover is not possible in this mode; therefore, if the principal fails, the mirror has to be promoted manually to serve the database. Due to synchronous transfer of the transactions and not being able to perform automatic failover, this operating mode is not recommended for normal applications.

Index

Index can be used to gain fast access to specific information in a database table. There are two types of indexes, clustered and nonclustered. In a clustered index, the physical order of rows in the table is the same as the logical (indexed) order of the key values. If an index is not clustered, the physical order of the rows in the table does not match the logical order of the key values. A clustered index usually provides faster access to data than a nonclustered index. A table can contain only one clustered index. Although, indexes can improve query performance, data entry can become slow. This is because every time data is entered in an indexed table, all indexes must also be updated.

Identity datatype

Identity is actually not a datatype, but is a property. When this property is assigned to any column, then each time SQL Server automatically creates sequential numbers for new records inserted in the table having the identity column.

For example the first record in the table would have an identity value of 1, and the next would be 2, then 3, and so on.

Identity columns might be included as a part of the primary key, therefore, it is important to avoid duplicate values in the identity columns.

A table is the collection of information arranged in rows and columns. Each intersection of a row and a column is known as a cell. A table is useful in representing numerical data.

A table is created with the CREATE TABLE statement and data is inserted into the table with the INSERT statement. The ADD CONSTRAINT clause in the ALTER TABLE statement is used to add a constraint to a column of an existing table.

In order to add a new column in an existing table, use the following syntax:

ALTER TABLE table_name ADD COLUMN column_name datatype NULL

In order to retrieve all the rows from a table and matching rows from other table, use the following syntaxes:

SELECT * FROM table1 LEFT OUTER JOIN table2 ON table1.primary_key_column_name=table2.foreign_key_column_name

SELECT * FROM table2 LEFT OUTER JOIN table1 ON table2.foreign_key_column_name=table1.primary_key_column_name CHECK constraint enforces domain integrity by limiting the values that are accepted by a column. In order to add a check constraint to a column, use the

ADD CONSTRAINT clause with the ALTER TABLE statement The DEFAULT constraint is a constraint in which a default value is given to a column if the value for that column is unknown. If a user does not provide any value for that column, the default value is automatically inserted. If a default value is not provided, then NULL is inserted. If a column does not allow NULL value and a default value is also not assigned for that column, an error is sent by the database engine. In order to create a computed column use the following syntax:

ALTER TABLE table_name ADD computed_column_name AS formula

Nonclustered index

A nonclustered index has the same B-tree structure as the clustered index. The index consists of a root page, intermediate levels, and a leaf level. The leaf level of a nonclustered index does not contain the actual data. It contains pointers to the data that is stored in the data pages. A nonclustered index does not physically rearrange the data.

OBJECT plan guide

An OBJECT plan guide matches queries that execute in the perspective of DML triggers, multi-statement table-valued user-defined functions, scalar user-defined functions, and Transact-SQL storedprocedures.

SET XACT_ABORT

SET XACT_ABORT is a T-SQL statement that specifies whether SQL Server automatically rolls back the current transaction when a run-time error is raised by a T-SQL statement. It has the following syntax:

SET XACT_ABORT { ON | OFF }

When SET XACT_ABORT is ON, and if a T-SQL statement raises a run-time error, the entire transaction is terminated and rolled back.

When SET XACT_ABORT is OFF, in some cases only the T-SQL statement that raised the error is rolled back and the transaction continues processing. The entire transaction may be rolled back even when SET XACT_ABORT is OFF, depending upon the severity of the error. OFF is the default setting.

Sysmail_sentitems

The sysmail_sentitems view contains one row for each message sent by Database Mail. When troubleshooting Database Mail, this view helps users identify the nature of the problem by showing them the attributes of the messages that were sent successfully. Messages are marked as sent by the Database Mail when they have been submitted successfully to an SMTP mail server.

sysmail_faileditems view

The sysmail_faileditems view contains one row for each Database Mail message with the failed status. This view is used to determine which messages were not sent successfully.

sysmail_allitems view

The sysmail_allitems view is used to see the status of all messages processed by Database Mail. This view helps users recognize the nature of the problem by displaying the attributes of the sent messages in relation to the attributes of the messages that were not sent.

sysmail_mailattachments view

The sysmail_mailattachments view contains one row for each attachment submitted to Database Mail. This view is used to get the information about Database Mail attachments.

Scalable shared databases

Scalable shared databases help to join a read only reporting database to multiple server instances over a storage area network. A reporting database is a read only database that is built from one or more production databases. It is used completely for reporting purposes. A reporting database must reside on one or more dedicated read-only volumes, to make it into a scalable shared database.

Snapshot replication

Snapshot replication distributes data at a specific moment. It does not monitor the modifications in data or schema. The entire snapshot is sent to Subscribers when synchronization occurs. The snapshot replication can be performed in the following conditions:

When data changes infrequently.

When small volumes of data are to be replicated.

When large volumes of changes occur over a short period of time.

sys.dm_fts_index_population dynamic management view

The sys.dm_fts_index_population dynamic management view displays information regarding the full-text index populations that are in progress currently.

The following table displays the meaning of each population type:

Population Type	Meaning
1	Full population
2	Incremental timestamp-based population
3	Manual update of tracked changes population
4	Background update of tracked changes

For example: The following query will return the incremental timestamp-based population currently active on the SQL Server.

SELECT*FROMsys.dm_fts_index_population WHEREpopulation_type=2

SQL plan guide

An SQL plan guide matches queries that get executed in the context of stand-alone Transact-SQL statements and batches, which do not form a part of any database object. T-SQL statements are submitted by an application by using the sp_executesql system stored procedure. SQL-based plan guides can also be used to match queries that parameterize to a specified form.

SET SHOWPLAN_XML ON statement

The SET SHOWPLAN_XML ON statement is used to capture the execution plan in a well-formed XML format that can easily be displayed graphically. It will not actually execute the statement but instead create the XML document for each statement. If a user selects the XML output, it will show the graphical representation. If the user then right-clicks within the plan, the XML document can be saved as a .sqlplan file.

SQL injection

SQL injection is a code injection technique that exploits a security vulnerability occurring in the database layer of an application. The vulnerability is present when the user input is either incorrectly filtered for string literal escape characters embedded in SQL statements or user input is not strongly typed and thereby unexpectedly executed. It is an instance of a more general class of vulnerabilities that can occur whenever one programming or scripting language is embedded inside another. SQL injection attacks are also known as SQL insertion attacks.

SQL injection is a code injection technique that exploits a security vulnerability occurring in the database layer of an application.

Stored procedure

A stored procedure is a collection of T-SQL statement or a reference to common language runtime (CLR) method that can return as well as take the user-supplied parameters. Procedures can be created for permanent use or for temporary use within a session as local temporary procedure, or global temporary procedure for temporary use within all sessions.

A stored procedure is a collection of T-SQL statement or a reference to common language runtime (CLR) method that can return as well as take the user-supplied parameters.

Transaction

A transaction is a logical unit or work, where related DML statements are grouped together. When a transaction is active, either all the statements in the transaction will complete successfully or none of them will run. This means that if any of the statements in the transaction fails due to any reason, the whole transaction will be rolled back. Transactions are ended by using the COMMIT or ROLLBACK statement.

Template plan guide

TEMPLATE plan guides are used to override the parameterization behavior for precise query forms. Users can create a TEMPLATE plan guide in any of the following situations:

The PARAMETERIZATION database option is SET to SIMPLE, which is the default setting, but on a class of queries users want forced parameterization to be attempted.

The PARAMETERIZATION database option is SET to FORCED, but there are queries compiled according to the rules of simple parameterization.

T-SQL table valued function

T-SQL table valued functions are used where view or table expressions are acceptable in T-SQL queries. Views are restricted to a single SELECT statement. A table valued function can also replace stored procedures that return a single result set. In the FROM clause of a T-SQL statement, the table returned by a user-defined function is referenced; however, stored procedures that return result sets cannot be referenced.

Scalar function is used to return a single data value of the type defined in the RETURNS clause. The scalar value results from a single function statement. Simple scalar functions have no function body but in multi-statement scalar functions the function body is defined in a BEGIN and END block containing a series of T-SQL statements that return a single value. The return type can be any data type except text, ntext, image, spatial, cursor, timestamp, and hierarchyID.

Scalar function is used to return a single data value of the type defined in the RETURNS clause. T-SQL table valued functions are used where view or table expressions are acceptable in T-SQL queries.

View

A view is a type of virtual table. The data accessible through a view is not stored in the database as a distinct object. Views are created by defining a SELECT statement. The result set of the SELECT statement forms the virtual table. A user can use this virtual table by referencing the view name in SQL statements in the same way a table is referenced. A view does not contain data of its own but derives (or dynamically displays) data from other tables or views on the basis of the query specified for the view. The tables from which a view derives data are known as base tables. Operations on a view affect its base tables.

The syntax for creating a view is as follows:

CREATE   VIEW   <VIEW   name>   AS   SELECT<attributes> FROM<Tablename>WHERE<condition>

A view can be used to speed up data retrieval you can add hint on query

In order to create a view use the following syntax:

CREATE VIEW view_name AS SELECT column1, column2 FROM table_name The SCHEMABINDING argument of the CREATE VIEW statement will prevent the deletion of a table. The CHECK OPTION argument forces the update of a view in accordance with its related tables.

Things to Practice: A Final Checklist

Microsoft's 70-452 test validates that an individual has the comprehensive set of skills necessary to perform a particular job role, such as database administrator or enterprise messaging administrator. MCITP certifications are built on the technical proficiency measured in the Microsoft Certified Technology Specialist (MCTS) certifications. Therefore, one can earn one or more MCTS certifications on the way for earning an MCITP credential. Candidates for this exam are IT professionals who design and plan business intelligence (BI) solutions by using Microsoft SQL Server 2008 BI tools.

Before taking the 70-452 test, you should practice the following:

- Prepare sub reports.

- Design a data acquisition strategy.

- Create appropriate SQL queries for an application (MDX Queries).

- Clean data.

- Perform column aliasing.

- Make a decision tree.

- Select a processing mode.

- Perform localization.

- Create a named set in MDX

- Analyze cube performance.

- Plan for scalability.

- Create on-demand-from-cache reports.

- Prepare a report history.

- Perform insertion over DML.

- Create cubes, projects, reports.

uCertify Test Prepration Software for Microsoft Exam 70-452

uCertify test preparation simulation software (PrepKit) is designed to efficiently help you pass the Microsoft Exam 70-452. Each PrepKit contains hundreds of practice questions modeled on real world scenarios. Each exam objective is covered with full explanations of key concepts and numerous study aids such as study guides, pop quizzes and flash cards help reinforce key concepts.

Installation is simple and no internet connection is required once you have installed the PrepKit. To download a free trial please visit:

Download link:

http://www.ucertify.com/exams/Microsoft/70-452.html

At the core of every uCertify Prepkit is our powerful PrepEngine that allows for a sophisticated level of customized learning. The folks at uCertify, understand that your time is important. We have created a unique blend of learning and test preparation, the foundation of which is working smarter. Years of experience has gone into the creation of detailed reference material that ensure your learning and practice questions that closely simulate real life technical problems to test your understanding of the subject. Our time tested and continuously improving methodology instantly gives you the benefit of separating the fluff from the real deal. Anticipating your needs and customizing the material to your strengths and weaknesses is at the core of our unique engine. We help you gain the skills you need not just to pass the test, but to actually use them on the job!

uCertify's Prepkits have numerous built-in Study Aids such as Flash Cards, Study Notes, Tagging and more reduce the burden of trying to determine how to sift through vast study material by providing refresher or quick reference at any time. Studies have shown this raises the confidence level of students. The student can on the fly, customize Practice tests and learning, such that the content meets their current levels of knowledge. Immediate, Gap analysis reports tell the student what they need to learn to perform better in a particular subject area. Context sensitive study material and tips help enhance a student's knowledge of a subject area, helping them truly learn the material. This helps improve student performance and productivity on the job for employees. The platform also has the capability for subject matter expertise to be captured and communicated in a consistent manner.

Top 12 features of our Award Winning Prepkits

1. Simple, intuitive, user-friendly interface

2. One click dashboard makes it easy to find what you need

3. Guided learning steps you through the process of learning and test preparation, including crucial information about the exam format and test preparation tips

4. Reference Notes and Study Guides organized according to the actual test objectives

5. Numerous study aids, including study notes, flash cards, pop Pop Quiz and more

6. Useful Technical Articles section contains information written by industry experts and How To's that help for easy look up to specific questions

7. Collaboration

8. Exhaustive practice questions and tests, starting with Diagnostic tests to determine your initial level

9. Learning and test modes

10. Customize your tests – decide how many questions, combine one or more topics of your choice, quiz yourself on a study note, increase the level of difficulty based on your performance at any point in time, even create a test based on the amount of time you have to take a test!

11. Feedback and assessment when you need it, including Gap Analysis that clearly indicate your areas of strength and weakness

12. Full length Final Practice test that closely simulates those on the certification exam to gauge your preparation level for the actual exam

Contact us

- **Fax:** 209 231 3841
- **US:** 800 796 3062
- **International:** 1 415 513 1125
- **India:** 532 244 0503
- **Sales:** sales@ucertify.com
- **Support:** support@ucertify.com

Useful Links

- **uCertify USA:** http://www.ucertify.com/
- **Download PrepKits:** http://www.ucertify.com/download/
- **PrepEngine Features:** http://www.prepengine.com/
- **uCertify Blog:** http://www.ucertify.com/blog

Made in the USA
Lexington, KY
07 January 2011